CROSS THE BRIDGE

PETE (K-SO G) KELLER

CROSS THE BRIDGE

2008

CROSS THE BRIDGE

INDEX

AUTHOR'S NOTE

There's a small dictionary in the back of the book, of words you may not know while reading. I feel it's easier to have your own glossary (one section to turn to, even if you want to study it before or after reading the book) than to cram the book heavily with footnotes. Most of these are everyday street words to us; some may be older, and only used every now and then, but the majority are commonly used. I feel these are vital to our communication.

Since street lingo (slang, as upper-class whites label it) changes yearly, I'm using only those prominent American street terms that have stood the test of time, and are not segregated, as some slang words are, changing from city to city.

As you read through the book, you'll notice I use quite a few parentheses. That's because I'm writing to you as if I'm talking to you, as if you were here with me. There are two things I try and stay away from: **Big Words** and **Statistics**. I feel that these are damaging to one's writing, and use them only when necessary. Believe me, and **I mean believe me,** from running a community newspaper, dealing with the mayor's office, community organizing, news and media, business meetings, mail from around the world, late-night library studies, homework, hands-on experience, college, networking, attorney guidance, architectural printouts, research, research, and more research, and fourteen years of prestigious writing, I have enough statistics to pack this entire book from front to back with blah! But statistical mumbo jumbo is boring, even if it's written (and presented) as interestingly as the author thinks. The same is true regarding cluttering a sentence with big words.

The problem is that a lot of white-collar society feels that it is necessary to write in as complicated a manner as possible, in order to achieve a level of importance. Why should we let these authors or journalists try to impress us with how much intricate (often unnecessary) information they've gathered rather than the message they're trying to get across? It's a backward step in American writing that we just recently (within the last sixty years) started doing. It's acceptable if you're talented enough to balance your love for writing with a statistical agenda, but it's rare that you give it the balance it deserves.

I need you to understand that when I'm referring to blacks and whites throughout the book, I tend to be specifically focusing on both ends of the financial pole, from upper-class whites (often including yuppies) to lower-class ghetto blacks. So don't take offense, middle-class white and black America.

Also, a lot of the time when I'm using "he," I'm referring to both genders, unless otherwise specified.

There will be times **throughout** the book that I will (subconsciously) play reverse roles so quickly through a sentence that whites will instantly be black and vice versa. Use it for your benefit. It's merely a helpful technique in my endeavor and a contribution to our goal.

While reading this book, you may feel stereotyped. Don't. There will be times when you'll say, "I don't act like that; that's not true." And these will be the times when you're probably right. However, that's what I'm trying to break: the stereotypes, the mental projection of races, and the thought that we all act the way we're supposed to. How are we supposed to act? Exactly. The book is not pinpointing anyone, it's reflecting everyone.

***

To those suburbanite moms in the boondocks: the curse words that are used in this book are used as forms of expression, forces of energy in speech that we as Americans simply use.

Mrs. Mom, I will admit that cursing in everyday speech can be tasteless, not to mention careless; that's why it's limited in this book. However, this book is aimed at the extreme radicals on each end of society and those in between. From the penitentiary to the White House, from the ghetto to you! Yes, you. So, understand that the majority of people, real people, are not like you—they're just not. We are a nation of struggle, and as your kids go to school in the morning, they curse; as your husband endures a long, agonizing day at work, he curses too; and moms, we've even heard you curse many times when you thought we didn't.

I realize there are efforts being made by countless programs, books, counselors, and workshops to stop children (and adults) from cursing. Profanity in America is as big as we make it, and apparently many people have approached it as a serious (self-inflicted) problem, so I shall handle it as such, out of respect. However, my intent is one of progress, for all of us, and cursing is neither the threat nor the cure. It is simply a beneficial aid in my writing with those who relate. If it takes those "bursts" throughout a realistic book to produce a positive outcome, so be it. If cursing ruins your perception of this book, then you've cheated yourself.

Read the book with an open mind. I'm counting on you, I'm depending on you, and I need you to do that for us—me and you. Remember, a mental slap in the face is what makes us Americans; it's better and does more good than a physical slap any day. Thus, the pen will continue to be mightier than the sword! Let us pull ourselves together as a nation. Ours is such a glorious nation; let us flourish as never before—all of us.

INTRODUCTION (ABOUT THIS BOOK)

I t's been hard as hell writing this book. I've been bouncing from place to place, had no computer, been incarcerated at times (which didn't stop the progress, though), had family problems (including deaths), been broke, been on house arrest, and basically put it off because I felt incapable of doing the job well. All writers get into a rut, but I simply quit writing; I felt it was unimportant in my life.

Why create this book? Well, to put it in basic terms, **enough is enough**. I'm tired of phony-ass remarks from each side of the racial barrier, criticizing how one operates, dresses, dances, drives, speaks, screws, smells, thinks, acts, looks, and communicates. Those on both sides of the fence have a preconceived notion of each other, distancing us. Why? Not so much "why isn't anything being done?" but "why are we progressing so slowly?" as to not have done anything sooner.

It seems as if nobody's coming forth to get this show on the road. As in all shows, there has to be a beginning. My beginning is looking at the problems. Yes, the problems Americans face are not like those of any other nation: our communities, cities, and states are so diverse in themselves that ideas, fads, slang, activism, racial unity, styles, and plight change from state to state. Our country's diversity lies within its mixture of people—and yet, instead of making the diversity a positive compliment, we've shunned it, making it the problem (not even knowing it), too scared to tackle it, feeling as if we don't know how. Why? What the hell is **our** problem?

Our problem is that those who don't know are too scared or lazy to make the effort, those who do know haven't come forward to help others, and those who want to know don't know where to begin or whom to go to. Our problem is that, instead of looking into the problem we've covered it up—we know it's there, but don't want to deal with it. Our problem is that we have a problem and won't deal with it. Our problem is that we've made a bigger problem out of the problem that we had better deal with! NOW! And the worst part is that our problem is really not a problem at all! That's our problem.

So here we are…facing supposed American problems. We will look at these problems, bearing in mind that many of them are simply people dealing with life, many of them are simply people dealing with each other, and many of them are just simple—too simple.

Picture yourself on a packed bus. There are forty other people on this bus; some standing, some talking, some laughing, some silent; men, women, and children of all ages. Some may have gotten on before others, and some may get off before others, but all are going in the same direction! Each person will perceive the bus ride differently, though they are all on the same ride. Children will stare at people or look out the window seeking entertainment, women will notice others' clothing styles and think ahead in planning, elders will be thankful if someone offers a seat, and men simply want off the bus! I've now obviously stereotyped someone as to what I believe they perceive. Right? Touché. And this is our problem, too; thinking for others before knowing them; preventatively assuming and generalizing their race, culture, and actions with what we see (and think) instead of what we know! There may be times when we are right, but most of the time we're not because we just don't know for sure—and we need to. It makes all the difference in the world. Whether or not a man facing the death penalty is guilty has to be based on raw facts, not on what we believe could have happened. This is critical.

One thing we do know is that we're all on the same bus (which represents life and where we **appear** to be heading, supposedly moving forward). Some will get off and leave before others, as others continue to board. But all will ride this bus. So respect that, understand that, and as others try and learn about you, in return do the same.

The title *Cross the Bridge* has been chosen because it represents the primary focus of this book and our humanitarian plight. A bridge links two sides together, the side you're on and the side you're going to. I look at it as being an "out with the old, in with the new" frame of mind. Sometimes the bridge itself is unstable and hard to get across, sometimes it's long, and sometimes **you** simply don't want to cross. However, in order to get to your destination, you MUST. Once you're on the other side, you've achieved your goal by crossing, and can continue your adventure.

Sound like a big deal? Over-exaggerated? Well, hey, it is for a reason! All BS aside, if we didn't have bridges we'd be screwed! Point-blank. I guess we take it for granted. Don't!

This book was designed to explain the problems so you can move ahead in thought. Cross your own bridge however the heck you want, but cross. Just remember: the bridge itself represents the problems, myths, gossip, assumptions, and preconceived notions. It's important that we deal with facts: facts on how ghetto youth live; facts on what you go through when being incarcerated; facts on black and white ideology; facts on the differences in religion and faith; facts on the differences in emotions. Then add your own facts into these for a final factual analysis.

We've started another decade (and are damn near done with it), but this one seems futuristic as we repeat "twenty-first century" in our minds! Our grandchildren will not know the '70s or '80s, or understand the simplistic value of the '90s. There was a lot of tension during 2000. Nearing the end of the year, predictions were made, bank accounts were closed, church congregations repented, babies were baptized, and uncertainties brought yet more uncertainties.

Though the world didn't literally blow up then, it had long ago blown up in people's minds, and will get as bad as we make it. People just don't know about one another, and this gap is what we're trying to bridge. Walk this bridge, talk this bridge, show others your bridge, and learn about theirs. And, most importantly, cross this bridge.

I'd like to thank you for being interested in reading this book—you've shown your leadership in crossing.

ADRENALINE

Adrenaline is a must in our American society.

Looking out of my seventh-story window while on house arrest in the Cabrini Green Housing Projects, I saw two teenage girls fighting! There's a large crowd around them and both girls had weapons; one had a broken bottle and the other a knife (which I later found out was a box cutter). Though family members of both girls were in the crowd, along with the mother of one, no one broke up the fight. Surprisingly, after falling in the dirt and rolling around, no one was cut, only clothes ripped, punches thrown, bruises made, and breasts shown. An hour and a half later, while looking out the same window, I saw the same two girls sitting together in the broken-down playground, drinking a forty ounce as their kids played.

Twenty minutes after that, looking out the same window, I saw a guy I know run into the building with a gas can. He poured the gas on his apartment door and lit it, while family members were inside! The fire trucks and ambulances came People were somewhat burned but escaped, and the apartment had disintegrated. The police caught him soon after.

Forty-five minutes after that, looking out my side window that faces the parking lot, I saw three detective cars pull up on the side of our building. They burst out of their cars, caught six men, handcuffed them to a pole, slapped them around, left, and came back ten minutes later only to let them go—supposedly, a weak-ass "scare tactic" to get them to talk.

Then the phone rang. It was an investigator from house arrest, questioning me on where I'd been for the last half hour! I told her I hadn't been anywhere (which I hadn't), but she demanded to know my whereabouts and squawked that the cheap plastic ankle bracelet couldn't be wrong. She then insisted on knowing my apartment number (which I knew she already had, but I gave it to her anyway) and hung up on me! So then I was nervous, looking out the window, feeling that they're coming to lock me up.

Twenty minutes after that, two dope fiends (whom I thought were the house arrest people) knocked on my door, out of breath, with four **deep dish** chrome rims for my truck; they only wanted three hundred dollars for all four! Which I didn't have. They then tried to sell me two pair of Victoria's Secret panties for my woman. Which I didn't want.

I brushed my teeth and was about to hit the sack when *bloogow!* came the first shot from under my window. Then *looga! looga! looga!* came three quick, roaring shots in return. I cut the lights (which is the norm whenever you hear shots in the projects, before going to the window), then peeked out. One man ran behind the other, but as they disappeared into the shadows it was hard to tell if it was a chase, so I waited for more shots.

Since no shots came, I hit the sounds (turned up my music) and was about to fall asleep, but heard the phone. My homie, John, who also lives in the building, was giving me the lowdown on the shots. As usual, it was another sleepless night; not because I **couldn't** sleep, but because I didn't want to—my adrenaline kept me up.

My community, as do many, seeks attention. People need to be noticed. There was a time when this night would have been outrageous to me, the night from hell, but now it's quite normal. I feel guilty at times that I need this adrenaline. In fact, I'm bored when there's no action as such. Adrenaline is a must in my life, as it is in yours and everyone else's.

Whites live in a society (more a state of mind, really) that tells them everything has to be limited: you can only have so much fun or it becomes ridiculous; you can only stress so much or you'll have a breakdown; you can't overdo your hobbies or it cuts into your personal life; don't overdo your personal life or it cuts into your work and business; and don't overdo your work and business or you won't have a life! Thus, you abide by this ethic, making your life as disciplined as possible. And though this can be looked upon as a positive endeavor (something that must be done in order to maintain results), it has its pros and cons.

The pros in having a structured life are as follows: being stable, you've finished school; finishing school, you've been offered a good working position; having a good working position, you've increased finances; increasing finances, you've moved up in society's standards bracket; in moving up, you've made new living arrangements, associates, plans, and experiences. You've bought things that you previously couldn't and you're still climbing the financial ladder of success.

The cons in having a structured life are as follows: your social life has been limited through the years; if you don't have a strong social life, your concept of people is limited; if your concept of people is limited, two things happen:

1. Others' endeavors seem less significant to you because it's all about self. The level of importance toward self (how you perceive yourself) interferes with your outlook on others. This usually happens with those who make a high salary.
2. You become harder and more disciplined since your free connection with people is limited; everything is about work, and work is related to structure, and structure is related to self.

Thus, you've become distanced from the humanitarian side of life because your balance is off, though you may not perceive it to be. With all the extra points you get from society by being what they expect you to be (and what you feel they want you to represent), your integrity has been damaged. Is it worth it? The pros and cons in having a white structured life seem irrelevant; yet how can they be when it's factual? And how does adrenaline fit in white society?

Whites often pay for adrenaline whether they know it or not. However, there's confusion that adrenaline portrays adventure. They think that, when going skydiving or bungee jumping, it's the sport itself they are interested in, when in actuality it's the adrenaline. They may know this subconsciously. And they'll pay for anything that offers this mental stimulation: hockey, laser tag, motor cross, drag racing, skiing, windsurfing, regular surfing, snurfin, roller coasters, and paintball!

Seeing that white-collar society is so structured (dare not anything be out of the norm), nothing spontaneous is offered during your daily routine. Thus, it's normal to seek this adrenaline that you feel you need—and you pay for it. It's all too easy, but this too can have its pros and cons.

The pro to this (seeking and paying for adrenaline) would be that it keeps you within society's guidelines, safe, and with the concept that you "get your daily dosage, then it's over with" mentality. Okay, and this is fine, but wow, it says something.

The con to this (seeking and paying for adrenaline) is that you've become rigid! No wonder blacks view whites as being stern, stiff, unrealistic, and sometimes robotic in character! With having to fit in (and pay) for adrenaline rushes, it shows that our lives have become **too** structured.

And it follows that as our white-collar yuppies become middle-aged, their standards of what adrenaline offers tells them that too much is not kosher, it's not proper (still relying on some type of mental system). Thus, they gear themselves to become satisfied with the more subtle events: opera, bowling, golf, theatre, and movies. So, having a white structured life is not irrelevant; bend the rules sometimes in a positive way and hold on to your integrity. It's worth it.

Blacks, on the other hand, can't possibly view adrenaline the same way. With no stability in the ghetto, mental rules and regulations are not those of whites. No long-term goals or immediate foundation to give the idea that you can be sidetracked from obtaining the goal, because you feel that you are as low as you can fall. You are already living in the bottom of society's barrel, where whites don't want to end up.

So to fill that structured void, you do what you have to in order to make it! With no need to go anywhere to pay for adrenaline incidents, you are surrounded with the opportunity to make your own, and it's not looked upon as how whites would view it—as a big deal or outrageous—it is simply a way of life! And yes, you too get invisibly hooked on the adrenaline.

On The Corner

One hot summer evening about five months ago, I was chilling on Cambridge and Locust, which is one of the corners in my hood. There's a stoop that sits four feet away from the corner, and I was sitting there with my friend Ace. As we kicked it about old times, cars rolled by beating their sounds, and people were out.

After ten minutes of sitting on the stoop, a man came by selling socks, incense, lighters, and barrettes. I bought a bundle of socks and Ace bought three lighters for a dollar. He handed the man a sawbuck and waited for his change, but the man started walking off. Ace hollered, "Hey! Hey, homie! Excuse me, player, where you going? I gave you a sawhead!" Ace and I jumped up as the old man picked up his pace. We caught him, went in his pockets, and took the accurate change.

Two minutes later (directly in front of us), one car bumped into another. The driver in the front jumped out with a bat and went to look at the damage. Though there was no damage, he was mad as hell and demanded that the driver get out of his car. The other driver did, looked at the damage, reached into his pocket, and gave the bat holder a hundred-dollar bill for his trouble—even though there wasn't a scratch. The bat holder, suddenly being spoiled, jumped on the idea that he could possibly get more money and started snapping again, waving the bat around! The other driver snapped back, "Man, what the fuck? I just gave your bitch ass a C-note for nothing. Just for your trouble, nigga! Man, keep talking and I'll take that shit back, what!" The bat holder, still holding on to the hundred-dollar bill, tried one more time to get some more money. "Man, how the fuck you gonna give me a hundred-dollar bill? This ain't enough for—" He was abruptly cut off by the other driver. "Bitch, you still talking shit? Fuck that!" he snapped, getting into his car. When the bat holder saw him getting into his car, he knew that meant one thing: he was strapped! So the bat holder dove into his own car and peeled off.

Ten minutes after that, three men were walking toward us (on our right) as three other men approached (on our left). As the two groups met up (about to walk by each other), one of the guys from one group stole on another from the other group! Instantly they were boxing (I found out later that they'd had bitter words the day before) and took the fight into the small street. None of their friends broke it up, as they went from boxing to wrestling, body-slamming each other on the hard concrete to the hoods of cars. They fought for ten minutes. Finally I saw blood, though I didn't know whose. Since they were blocking traffic, their friends didn't give a damn, and they were all over cars belonging to people they didn't know, I went to break it up. Trying not to get any blood on me, I grabbed the big brotha who was currently on top, smashing the other's head into the windshield of a Chevy, and pulled him back. "You lucky K-So saved your ass, bitch-ass nigga, or I'da killed your ass!" he hollered, as I pushed him onto the sidewalk and told his friends to grab him. After the other guy took off his shirt and wiped his bloody face, he came to talk to me, explaining what had happened the day before. After he left, with the crowd still lingering and recapping the fight, someone hollered out, "Yo! Yo! what they hitting for?" And a dice game kicked off. The dice game went up to twenty dollars a fade and fifty a hit. A shorty walked off winning twelve hundred. An hour into the game, the police rolled up and broke it up. The guys moved half a block down the street into a cut.

As the guys (and girls) moved down the street, the "dog pack" came out. These are the people in the project who own dogs and fight their pit bulls every chance they get. Everyone knows the name of each of these dogs from their wicked fights, which often lead to death! Two of the dogs fought right in front of us, and bets were placed. The crowd grew, and finally a bright reddish dog named Big Red won, tearing the neck of the other into applesauce. Ace popped the trunk of his uncle's car, pulled out a sheet, and we wrapped the dog in it before throwing him into a dumpster.

We then heard the sound of the ice-cream truck getting closer. As it pulled up, the kids bum-rushed it! There was chaos in the crowd, as all the kids wanted to be the first. A nine-year-old boy felt on the butt of a twelve-year-old girl, so she turned around and smacked him. Since he was in front of his boys, he had to fight back, which he did. As the two fought, the man in the ice-cream truck, seeing that they were stopping his money, jumped out of the truck to break it up. But as soon as he jumped out, three of the boys jumped in and drove off with the truck! The man ran after his truck, falling twice. Ace and I busted out laughing so hard that I had cramps.

Then the wino click came stumbling down the street. When they got in front of us, holding their pints of Thunderbird, one of them said, "Okaaay, dig, we gonna do this song for yooou, K-So, and your guy Ace, who's in da place, with da cool face! Just tell us if we can win at the Apollo! Okaaay?" The four of them busted out their version of "Under the Boardwalk" by the Drifters. One man kept coming in too soon, or at least that's what the so-called leader of the group said, so he didn't pass him the Thunderbird. This angered the man, so he stopped singing altogether. The leader pulled out a small army knife and threatened to cut him. The man was so mad at not being allowed to hit the Thunderbird that he walked directly into the knife—it went straight in him, through his tank top! He fell to the ground with the knife lodged in his chest. I called for an ambulance on my cell. After the ambulance left, I started walking home. I had had enough for one night.

Ace walked halfway with me. We were trippin' on all the shit that happened on that corner, and it showed us the search for adrenaline the ghetto holds in great demand that is offered freely for the taking; young to old were taking it!

My friend Ace was killed the following month.

Analysis

Though adrenaline is not technically an emotion (it is a hormone that causes a physical reaction) it is connected to each of our emotions, and is often more powerful than love because it piggybacks onto every emotion, including love; it's versatility through life's perception is practically equal to emotion itself! Adrenaline can be offered through love or hate, it can be conjured through a song or watching sports, it can be delivered by participating in sports or singing a song. It's present at the miracle of birth and at your death bed. There's adrenaline in being locked up, going to work, making love, being faithful, and keeping faith! There's adrenaline in life.

How cultures perceive it and obtain it simply depends on the lifestyle. So let us just think and focus on the **lifestyles** that crave the adrenaline, because we realize that everyone needs it. So, how they're obtaining it says more than anything, because it's not the adrenaline itself we need to focus on.

Remember, like anything, adrenaline can be overdone. Thus, people get hooked and it's never enough; you only skydived once this week; not enough drugs; you and the boss only had two arguments; you're tired of catching your lover in lies, but you accept it because it adds stimulation (whether good or bad). You crave it, you have to have it—adrenaline is a must. Also, you get just as bored mentally if you don't have it physically. Americans listen to gossip, watch talk shows, and read tabloids because they offer this mental adrenaline. We'd rather creatively run wild with our minds than go the boring factual route.

So I want you to notice adrenaline. Really. Look at how you, yourself, obtain it. What do you do to get it? How much? In looking at this, you can find out more about yourself. Then, think about others and what they do to get it. In dealing with and understanding each other, it's the little things that we all see from different viewpoints that matter.

BALANCE

Balance in life is what gives us the opportunity to handle life. Everything and everyone becomes a part of the balance, whether positive or negative. While writing this particular chapter, I'm incarcerated here in Chicago's Cook County Jail. Though I'm upset, disappointed, and mad as hell because I have a "possession charge" that the cops put on me (yes, it sounds like TV when you hear about cops putting drugs on someone, but this shit happens for real—with crooked cops—when you don't have a lot of money), I still have to remind myself that everything happens for a reason, so I'm certain that positive will prevail. In the meantime, life goes on and in here it's all business; nothing's personal (so they say!). However, every day in here something kicks off between two men that definitely appears personal. And is.

Too, the deck I'm on has almost "gone up" six times, meaning the gangs have been at a standoff (gang members jumping out of their bunks, throwing their shoes on, grabbing their shanks, and getting ready to throw down when they hear a confrontation between two opposing gang members), and the only one who would even attempt to get in the line of fire and break it up was—who else?—me. Tension stays in the air for days after this happens, because guys don't want to be caught off guard in the event that the deck suddenly goes up for real. Thus, people stare at each other, watch each other, and there's an annoying silence, although the deck is noisy with the hustle and bustle. Inside (themselves), gang members invisibly search for the fight, because there's adrenaline in chaos. That's too bad.

The reason I don't let shit go down is because I've been through it way too often and realize that three things happen once a deck "goes up":

1. At least two or three people get seriously hurt and sent to the hospital (hopefully it won't be you).
2. There's always a snitch in the crowd who's going to tell on whomever started it—sometimes it's even one of the gang

members—thus, you and whoever else have a new case added to the case you're already locked up for!

3. If you can break up the fight before it starts, usually the same two who got into the confrontation will be cool the next day.

Besides, it's too obvious that tearing up the deck won't bring us results, just a bunch of bullshit. We're already locked up, why make it worse?

My bunk lies between those of two opposing gang leaders. One has a prosthetic leg and is constantly on the go, the other never leaves his bunk—people come to him. The three of us do what is necessary to keep peace throughout the building, let alone on our deck. The gang leaders don't want to admit it, but I know their presence has brought the tension to their foot soldiers, all wanting to impress their leader by showing him that they ain't no punks!

So, though we try to instill peace, it's a struggle—not just between the foot soldiers, but I notice a little competitiveness between the leaders. I suppose that's why I'm the only one jumping to break up shit, because they are of the mentality that if one side wins it's a triumph, rather than the fact that if one side wins, we both lose, because we're still hurting each other. And when we get done fighting, the officers will come in and fuck us up even more, then send us to the hospital while blaming it on the gangs! Though the leaders do a job to a certain extent, if you're not going to do the job 100 percent, then push to the side (step the fuck down) and let someone else step up—someone who can bring the balance needed.

One way you can relate to balance is thinking about the job of a parent. A parent has the job of being a mediator, a referee, someone who gives balance to the children—who's right, who's wrong, equal respect, equal love, equal sharing and advice. But that's one-sided balance (the balance that we offer others), which is a side effect of our own balance.

Balance in life can be symbolized best by the Chinese yin and yang emblem. ☯ The black and white are opposites, yet together, swirled into one, yet separate, with opposite-colored specks on both sides. This shows perfect balance. Our daily lives are supposed to create this same balance, with the things we do, the people we meet, the places we go, and the way we think. Our own balance consists of how we perceive life, and the positive or negative forces we work with or against, to live it. Remember, life is flawless; there are no mistakes in life. Humans are merely creatures here to embrace it and participate; how you embrace and participate depends on you. Everything you view depends on how you view it. Just because you feel there's always a negative with a positive, that's not true. The balance is not positive versus negative, the balance is with the positive. You have an equal amount of negativity that can enter if you allow it, and vice versa. Balance can work for you or against you. "Murphy's Law" can be considered by some as being true, and I'm quite sure it can be if you've allowed negative thoughts, and related negative actions, maneuver your life. If you are constantly allowing yourself to get into the rut of thinking and believing that all bullshit will happen regardless, then it will—because your mental balance has been thrown off.

CONFUSED BALANCE

The other day, I received a copy of my friend Billy Wimsatt's book *No More Prisons*. I literally read it while walking around my dorm. I was touched by the message, proud of my friend, and engulfed by the concept. For those who still haven't read *No More Prisons*, it's targeting "the prison industry, urban life versus suburban sprawl, self-education and home-schooling, hip hop and urban leadership, and cool rich kids and philanthropy." These five components are in relation to each other and Upski (Billy Wimsatt's nick name) discusses them in detail, giving you a look at why they are related.

After reading the entire book in two hours, I collapsed on my bunk glowing with triumph! My friend had finished his second book. The book had meaning to me and tugged at my heart. I was so touched by his accomplishment that I wanted others to read it—hell, I wanted everyone to read it—but something happened!

As I had been pacing the dorm while reading, everyone had noticed how into the book I was, plus the title, *No More Prisons*, had caught their eyes, so everyone was interested in checking it out. Upon finishing, I eagerly handed the book to the first person I saw, who accepted it just as eagerly. But as I passed by his bunk an hour later, I noticed the book on the floor, with a bookmarker still in the first chapter. This pissed me off, so I grabbed the book and passed it along. The second guy was from the ghetto, and did the exact same thing—and so did a third, fourth, fifth, sixth, and seventh—until two days had passed and I was dumbfounded.

I decided to go a different route. Before giving the book to someone, I sat down with that person and explained what I felt to be the important aspects of the book, along with personal highlights—still the same results! In fact, I would let some people hold on to the book for two and three days at a time, only to find the book once again on the floor, with only a few pages read.

So I decided to ask questions. I went back to those who had read only a chapter and asked them why. I wanted them to answer honestly, without feeling as if they were offending me or being mean. Many of them said that the book had nothing to do with them, others said it didn't interest them, but a few of my close friends seemed more honest. They said, "Man, the way he's writing, I don't understand what the fuck he's talking about. This boy's on some weird way-out shit." I was hurt, but I appreciated their honesty.

It seems that because of what he wrote—possibly how he wrote it, the words he used, his humor and plight—it immediately said he was unclear, different, or not understandable, thus shutting off their interest. Without the interest in finishing the book, it became a chore to even pick it up. This saddened me; it shows how something can be positive for one person, yet negative to another, thus showing you what "confused balance" is all about.

When positive and negative forces impact balance, it's sometimes easy to sway either way, because this is when our minds have all the responsibility of making the decision. If people look up and see me reading a bright, flashy book with the title *No More Prisons* in bold letters, they're apt to be encouraged to read it! But once they get a taste of it, and what they perceived turns out to be something else—at that moment they can change positive into negative and never finish the task at hand. Have you ever had a friend try to get you to go on a blind date, or go camping? If we've had a bad experience with these, a bad thought about them enters our minds, immediately closing the door to the positive. The blind date could've been great, the camping trip could've been rewarding, but we confuse the balance by not allowing the experience to happen. Don't let negative thoughts limit your balance.

BATTLING BALANCE WITH BIG RAY

The hardest part of my incarceration thus far has not been dealing with my loss to the streets, it's not been dealing with the guards, or even my case. The hardest part of my incarceration has been dealing with Big Ray. Big Ray is a six-foot four-inch white guy. He's taken from people all his life, never giving shit in return—ever! He's been on this deck almost a month, and not a day goes by that I don't want to kick his ass. He came to this deck because he couldn't make it anywhere else in the county jail, and I know why.

When Ray first walked through the door, there was an arrogance about him, but it was even more evident—as he walked over to a small white guy, opened his mouth, and demanded, "Hey, someone give me a square"—that he was a bully. There was one problem, and you could see it in his posture, hear it in his speech, and catch it in his movements. Ray was slow. He'd been in a couple of accidents and had hurt himself, but that hadn't changed his attitude for the better, it had only made it worse. Ray got high off crack, he'd torn his ass with his family, and now he was in here, demanding attention.

It got to the point that he'd literally follow people, practically on their heels, making them listen to his problems. Since people knew that I had the most patience and respect in the building, they came to me with the problem. At first, I pulled Ray into the bathroom and explained what not to do, but he'd start again later that night. Then Ray started making scenes, by getting loud and calling guys "bitches" and "hoes," which to many a man are fighting words. He'd gone the limit.

My problem was that, though I wanted to whoop Ray myself, I couldn't and wouldn't let anyone else put their hands on him! In fact, I made it my job to put him in check daily. But as his attitude worsened, I saw the inevitable; it was only a matter of time. This made me mad—mad as hell at Ray for not seeing how much I was going out on a limb for him.

Every day I walked and talked with Ray, trying to get him to understand that he was fucking up, and every night he'd wait until I was in bed to start something. I'd have to leave the bed, rush down the aisle, and save him from attack. I dreaded the thought of him. It became personal, and I plotted how I was going to bust his shit, myself! There was already enough tension in here dealing with the gangs, then we had others who weren't in gangs who'd have their own problems and snap out, and I'd have to deal with them, also. Big Ray was more than a recurring problem, he became a threat! My battle for balance became a struggle.

Big Ray knew what he was doing. Though his actions and movements may have been slow, he was smart and taking advantage of people with his size. Too, I felt he was taking advantage of me and the protection I offered. The sight of him sickened me, until one day, I woke up with the realization that today was the day. The first problem Big Ray started, I was going to lay the Foo Fops on him! The entire day I was on pins and needles, a cougar waiting to leap. By eight o'clock that night, I could take it no longer and went to my bunk to think. People don't understand what tension, what chaos, and what pressure surrounds inmates. But through all the mayhem, I caught myself. Let me explain.

As I sat and wrote this, there were fifty men around me. Someone had just stolen a radio from the guards (the remix of "Thong Song" was playing), the movie *The Green Mile* was blaring on the county's movie channel, there was a dice game in the bathroom (with arguing, of course), a gang meeting in the back on one side, on the other side a weed circle, by the windows were the Hooch Heads, brothers were arguing on the card table, and brothers were hollering into the phone because they could barely hear! And this was rehabilitation. So anyway, the noise level was unbearable, people were already ready for an excuse to let out tension by fighting—and Big Ray didn't care. The nicest of old ladies would have told me to kick his ass a long time ago. So as I sat on my bunk, I took all I had in my power to bring myself to a realistic level. A level that dug deep into reality and blocked out the hate, commotion, and hostility. I had to come to terms that, in being a man, I was going to have to make it my damn obligation to hold on, my obligation to make it work with Big Ray. Not trying to baby-sit him, but to do whatever it took to pull him up, because if I gave up, then it was opening the door to negativity and defeat. If I let somebody else put their hands on him, I was still losing; so Big Ray became my personal task. I just had to try harder, which **was** harder. I just knew that while writing this I would say, "Today I could take no more and whooped Big Ray." But every day I pushed harder to stand on his big ass, keeping him in the guidelines.

The other day, I woke up at 4:30 a.m. and had to pee; with cold in my eyes, I staggered to the washroom. Upon getting there, I saw and smelled a cloud of smoke that I knew was cocaine. Inside the washroom stood Ray, smoking a primo, paranoid as fuck. All my senses became alert, and my skin and the hair on my arms and back stood up like a porcupine! I grabbed Ray by the throat, pushing him against the wall; I took the laced cigarette out of his hand, threw it in the toilet, and stormed out. I couldn't believe it. I had done everything right, everything true and positive, and where had it led me? I wanted to just go off. I wanted to snap, and wake up everyone and tell them to take turns kicking his ass! I wanted to join in! I wanted to take a broom and crack his dome! But what did I do? I went to my bunk and lay there in the dark, and focused.

I awoke the next morning as if nothing had happened. I realized what I was up against. Maybe I could help Big Ray, and maybe I couldn't, but the bottom line was that I wasn't going to let his presence or plight throw off my balance.

Wherever we go (even in jail), we are faced with negative people who cause negative thoughts and actions. When we get rid of one negative factor, another comes in. So while battling balance during a negative issue seems hard, it is mandatory in order for you to maintain your plight. I felt that I had every right to beat up Big Ray, not just for all he'd put me through, but for what he was doing to himself. But I didn't. And maybe he needed a good ass-kicking, as long as it was done for the right reason and by the right person. I don't know what it would have accomplished, but I knew that it should have been the least of my worries while I was there.

ESSENCE BALANCE

People who are bilingual have essence balance, relating to and communicating with those of different nationalities. Jail and prisons have essence balance (whether people know it or not, with race relations) because whites, Latinos, and blacks get along. No doubt. The news and media only glorify racial incidents when they seem big or when someone dies, but even then it's usually not racial! Jails and prisons are quite the opposite; this is where races live among one another, all as inmates just trying to do their time. Even in the most racially talked about maximum prisons, the inmates realize that they are a target for the news and media to exploit, but they don't give a damn about that, just in doing what they have to in order to survive.

We take a lot for granted with our five senses in balance. If you watch a blind man, you notice how strong his other senses have become, which in turn gives him a strong sense of essence balance. A child has nearly perfect essence balance because negative thoughts are just beginning, responsibilities are fresh, and the willingness to give and share is plentiful.

To have the essence of balance is also worked into your daily schedule. If you organize your love life, job time, eating habits, entertainment, and social endeavors to what you feel is the most beneficial strategic schedule for you (and you're satisfied with it), then your essence in balance is working. However, there's also a downside to balance in the working schedule. Often in society, we end up following others' working schedules because we have to, thus making the best we can. For instance: If you're locked up and the prison has a schedule that everyone has to follow, then your balance might be stable as far as daily routine, but your personal essence may be off. Sometimes society makes us feel like we're locked up (even our jobs create this feeling), so our essence (which means "spirit," for those who still haven't caught on) becomes damaged. Maintain your essence; don't let your work schedule or personal life disturb your positive being, no matter where you are!

EARTHLY BALANCE

Since we live in what seems to be an ever-changing world, we have to remember that it is we who dramatically change, and because of this there is a 360-degree human domino effect continuing the balance that we are all a part of, worldwide. Thus the phrase "what goes around comes around" is valid because it literally is. Human connection is more physical than we think, more mental than we know, and more necessary than we're willing to admit. Earthly balance latches to physical balance, which activates our positive essence by the good deeds we do for others!

While in here, I've helped two men get their GED and helped three others get started on reading. To see their progress motivates and encourages my positive essence! The feeling of helping others is of this world, and anything of this world, as I said before, is perfect. Do something good for someone and don't tell a soul. This in itself is a natural high and will show you how powerful earthly balance can be.

PERFECT BALANCE

There's one last piece to the puzzle I'd like you to think about.

When you're doing what is necessary to achieve perfect balance—meaning your essence is strong, your thoughts are continuously positive, your determination overwhelming, your love expressive, your attribute triumphant, your words meaningful, and your presence inspiring—you will achieve what people refer to as "the high of life" or a "natural high." Since there is no specific name for this, we shall give it a short title right now; we will call this PB, for "Perfect Balance."

When the force of PB enters your life, there is no other emotion comparable, because PB handles all of your emotions, all of your actions, all of your encounters, and all of your worries. With PB you become the captain of your ship; so keep flying high!

Last week when I went to court, I sat in the bullpen with nine other men, listening to their problems and cases. And although I listened and advised, I was still a little concerned about my own case. Suddenly, the guards brought up a tenth man. As soon as the bars closed behind him, something else opened.

The man's name was Roberto; he was Italian and Puerto Rican (which he kept telling everyone), and definitely a PB client! He talked to all of us—some in Spanish, most in English—and lit up the room as everyone listened. He let us know that he was high on life, which I found intriguing, because he explained it in his own way while explaining his stolen car case. Today was his trial and he wasn't worried about the judge, how much time he was facing, or anything.

Roberto explained his own plight (what PB meant to him), why it was important to understand that everything happens for a reason, and that our job is to roll with the punches and remain positive. He claimed that everything was a test; even if you didn't want to look at it like that, you had to remember this in the back of your mind, even if you hated it or didn't give a damn, you had better respect it. Though his logic may not suit everyone, he was on the right track and it worked for him. That's what balance is all about: Finding your personal essence and making it work for you.

Roberto went out there (into the courtroom, in front of the judge) with more than a positive attitude—he went out there with PB. He was humble, yet radiant; he was patient, yet determined; and he had peace of mind. The judge, the jury, even the state's attorney came to realize that Roberto was innocent, and he beat the case. He came back into the bullpen and we prayed together. All of us.

This morning, the guards woke us up at 7:30 a.m. to go outside to the yard! Nobody knew the night before that we were going and that it was mandatory—we had no choice. I had washed the night before and all my socks were still wet. I rushed around the dorm trying to get a dry pair of socks from anybody. Everyone's stuff was either dirty or wet, so I decided to throw my shoes on my bare feet. As I turned to grab my shirt, someone tapped me on my shoulder.

"Hey, I heard you need a pair of socks. These are brand-new and I haven't worn them yet. Keep them, they're yours."

I already knew the voice as I turned around to take the socks. It was Big Ray. And not only was he appreciative that I took them, but he continued, "My mom's birthday is this week. Could you help me write her a letter? It would mean a lot to me." I stood there, stuck for a moment, then looked up at him and said, "Sure, Ray, I'd be glad to."

VISUAL EFFECTS (AFFECTS)

This was a hard chapter for me to write, because it hurts me to say what I'm about to say, but we must face it head-on.

We as Americans need "thick lens" glasses because how we see each other is not how we see each other. People see one another as transparent, on both sides. When I say transparent, I'm talking about how one views another as simply see-through, not there—invisible.

When blacks and whites are in public and see one another, it's as if they don't see one another. Walking down the street, blacks only pay attention to other blacks—their hairstyles, clothing, and partners. The only time they pay attention to whites is if there has to be physical contact or communication with them, or if they're with other blacks (such as in the workplace, where whites and blacks will interact with and often have a semi-relationship because of the workplace.)

On the reverse side, whites also only notice blacks if there has to be a transaction or communication. But furthermore, it's as if they don't count in this thing called life here in America (on both sides), as if the other is not real, literally unimportant, and unrealistic on what we feel society is based upon. (Meaning, that when we think about America and our personal immediate future other races aren't fixed into this preconceived ideology-until interactions occur.) What makes up your idealistic perception of things is based upon your background and culture, and how I identify that is simply by viewing you. Therefore, I immediately close my door to you upon sight, as being a nonmember of my society! The problem is that we all do this, to a certain extent, each and every one of us! Some may do it worse than others, but we all do it!

What happens is that there are so many in our own race that we don't deal with, wouldn't deal with, or can't imagine dealing with, that we couldn't possibly waste the energy even thinking about dealing with another race! We have the punk rockers, the drug addicts, the politicians, the gays, the lesbians, the overweight, the nasty snot-nosed gal at the corner store, and whatever else we feel guilty about and intimidated by. In truth, everyone fits into a class by someone else's standard, including us. So here we are, chopping up our own race, and along comes another. Instead of dealing with them as we would want to be dealt with, we immediately size them up by visual contact, compute them out with the more solid notion and past experience, and within an instant we have made an analysis. *It's too far-fetched to deal with*! We instantly realize. We all do this.

Then there are reverse roles on both sides that can be just as damaging, if not more so, where blacks and whites live a lifestyle completely stereotypical of the other race. Whites who live in the realm of black culture and society tend to dismiss white people as being unrealistic and accounted for in society. Blacks who live in the white world tend to stay in the white arena only, rarely dealing with other blacks. The only reason I say this can be more damaging is because, as humans, what we seek is balance. We need balance! Balance is what gives us peace of mind and stabilizes our stressful lives. These people who do reverse roles feel that they somehow have to master being the other stereotype.

When white youth act supposedly black, they do it in all the fields blacks are stereotyped in: street clothes, with the baggie, sagging look or the clothes that the rappers wear and promote; basketball (and it's not the fact that they're playing basketball, it's how they play it); and what they say ("Yo! Dog! Did you see dat shit, nigga? I'm the new Michael Jordan, fool."). And though this is street talk, they are using this the wrong way, simply as a form of stereotypical blackness. Rap music becomes law, every rap record that's "in" is learned backward and forward, and no other types of music are listened to, ever, even if they are liked. What comes to mind as a good representation of this would be a character in Danny Hoch's "Jails, Hospitals & Hip Hop" called Emcee Enuff. Try and find the CD, its between-the-lines message makes for some interesting listening.

On the adult level of this, white adults who want to be completely in the black arena often don't do it for the right reasons, because being in the so-called black arena should simply mean participating, learning, enjoying, and having fun. They do it as a form of feeling sorry for blacks or to fill a void in their own lives, thinking that they're being good Samaritans or defending a just cause.

Black adults, on the reverse side, feel that it's a standard of power or a level that they supposedly have to reach in white society to be accepted and successful; the opera, ballet, dinner banquets, and more, which seem to come with an amount of money. Bear in mind that I'm referring to a small percentage of "Reverse Roles" (12 percent).

However, the majority of whites who act street are truly from the streets, and the blacks who act proper have a nice income and many white friends because they've chosen to, not because they feel they have to. Thus, they are genuine.

Reverse roles are not the problem, though; in fact, they're more of the solution. The problem is the concept and what it offers the "12 Percent Reverse Role Recipient." The recipient has stereotyped a race and culture with their perception of what they feel that race has to offer, instead of what truly is. In doing this, you've thrown off your balance because you've closed the door to your own race. You've already taken the first step in opening your acceptance to another race, why blow it by overdoing it? Learn to balance the two, or three, or four, or five! Master your makings.

(WHO YOU ARE?)

When you get processed into the county jail, you are asked a ton of questions, including what race you are. The same thing happens when you fill out an application for a job, credit card, Social Security card, bank loan, birth certificate, etc. I understand that the government says it needs to know for statistical purposes, and employers leave that area optional, but we're so used to answering this question it's implanted within our subconscious to already expect it. What is Tiger Woods mixed with? What is Steven Segal mixed with? What is Prince mixed with? What is the damn problem? Why do people feel they need to know? Hello! Why are our brains invisibly demanding a response? Is it that we're still trying to find the perfect race? That when we see someone we like or dislike, we immediately need to know their makeup? Why are we so stuck in such a primitive ideology? Why do we continue handicapping our insights? Why? There are a number of reasons people will say they'd like to know, but I will tell you the two main factual reasons:

1. People feel comfortable when they can label you; it brings satisfaction to their unknowledgeable brains, constantly seeking answers to file data.

2. People have mistakenly made a connection between race and identity. With this connection (which has been perceived over the years with their encounters and hearsay on different races), they can decide whether they'll approve or disapprove of you before they get to know you.

I'm tired of people asking me, "What are you? Black, white, Spanish, or mixed?" Interview after interview, "What are you?" Meeting after meeting, encounter after encounter, I'm asked this same damn question until I start feeling sorry for those who ask. It's as if I can physically count the seconds until they ask. I can tell by their expressions when they want to ask; the shit is funny! When those who want to ask sense my humor, they usually don't ask.

Catch yourself the next time you look at someone and think, "I wonder what he or she is? I wonder what his or her racial identity is?" Ask yourself, what's the big deal? What is it that makes you so curious to know? Does their visual effect spark such a flare that you need to know what race or nationality they are? Wouldn't it be the shit to see people for their actions instead of their looks? Really.

We say this and we teach this to our kids, but how many people actually (and honestly) do it? How many of us live as if a blind man? A blind man sees through people's actions and words; he can't see color or physical makeup, but he feels entity and kindness; more or less, he's aware of the negative and positive, and tunes into them as he sees fit. Let's get our act together and tune in like the blind man, who in actuality is a step ahead of us.

In going one step further (to show how primitive we are), let's quickly look at the invisible spectrum of what we perceive to be race—in order to ask—are you black, white, mixed? In order to bring ourselves to ask people this question, our perception of their (or what we feel to be) majority race must be altered. If you perceive a white male to be fair-skinned with straight hair (whether blond or brown) and one of those is altered—for instance, the hair; let's say it's wavy and coarse—then suddenly, something in our minds has a hard time computing until we categorize, and we have to ask. Therefore, whites have to look white and blacks have to look black (they had better have a dark complexion and what we feel to be is black people's hair), or they have to be mixed! It's only right! Right? Our minds have already perceived races, and the bit of altercation calls into question our very own perception.

(WHO'S REALLY ON TRIAL?)

The same thing with the whole O.J. Simpson trial—and we're not debating whether or not he did it, but the effect it had on society. O.J. (whether realizing it or not) put blacks in the realm of being caught between a rock and a hard place; and too, opened the door for private (and personal) gain for black organizations that would not have dealt with him otherwise.

Blacks who never knew (or even cared) who O.J. was instantly found themselves in the middle of a controversy. And more attention from black America (and when I say black America, I'm talking about black power movements, black grassroots organizations, and those personal profit gainers!) was focused on the issue that he was black, instead of what was right or wrong.

So, O.J.'s skin color (again, whether or not he did it) opened the door for a negative racial issue here in America. What maddened white America was not that he was black and got away with injustice, as those many black organizations tried pinpointing, it was the fact that many perceived him to be somewhat guilty in their eyes, and because of his wealth and his "dream team," he manipulated his way out of what appeared to be murder or a link to murder, regardless of race. What got O.J. the attention was that he was truly liked by mainstream America: sports commentator, actor, and ex-football star. They liked O.J. and found it hard to believe he was in that situation, as they watched him run during the Bronco chase! Thus, they felt cheated. They'd been deceived by an emotion. That's what any actor, radio personality, or entertainer offers us, an emotional response. We're tied to them, and O.J. severed his personal link to us. Then it gets thicker, because when you're deceived, you get upset; when you're upset, you talk about it; and if you're white and you talk about it to someone black, the immediate response or impression is that it bothers you because you're prejudiced. But if two blacks are talking about it, different angles pop up: who's more realistic, who's more pro-black, who's more the detective and analyst, who's more the womanizer, and who just doesn't give a fuck. If two whites are talking about it, they too can be more honest and bring up points that they might feel uncomfortable talking about with blacks, because they don't want them to think they're prejudiced. And vice versa, with blacks talking about it with whites, because if they side with Nicole Brown, then they have the feeling of selling out or simply agreeing with the white person because they're sucking up or kissing ass. What a crock of shit we allow ourselves to feel, what a phony front we put on! But it gets deeper.

Since many Americans are prone to just use the visual effect along with the negative help of the news and media, the O.J. case becomes a "heated" black and white issue. With this happening, a lot of whites who buy into the visual effect look upon it literally as a win for blacks, as far as how they feel blacks perceive it. This too is false, because blacks don't feel this way. In fact, every single black person I've talked to, from the ghetto to Wall Street, isn't concerned with whether or not O.J. did it—they simply don't give a fuck. A "win" for black America is seeing Dominique Dawes take home a gold medal; a positive black senator or congressman; a black inmate on death row getting released due to DNA evidence; or the smile Michael Jordan gives when winning another ring and M.V.P. of the Year. So in actuality, a lot of wins for black America are wins for Americans in general. Do you see now how the O.J. issue went deeper than most realized or understood?

Here's a thought that would put things more into perspective on both sides of the racial barrier. Imagine if the issue was entirely black (everyone involved); it would still have the same publicity because of O.J. being the icon that he is, there would still be a woman involved and a male friend (possibly gay, for the rights movement), and I guarantee you it would have had as much publicity, if not more, because we could pick sides for right and wrong reasons instead of black and white ones. We could say how we felt O.J. cheated us without taking the blame for being prejudiced, blacks could express their anger on either side, women's organizations could express their anger without appearing prejudiced, and we all could talk about it openly and honestly.

This alone shows us that we as Americans are still climbing the ladder to dealing with our racial issues. Not only do we not know how, but we're not being honest with ourselves in saying that we don't know how. Humans learn a great deal about self through traumatic incidents.

Let's take the O.J. case and analyze its racial content with sincere efforts toward self first, then how others may perceive it concerning their persona, background, career, financial status, gender, and lastly race (in this order). Once we have our own personal perspective in order and seriously consider another individual's perspective (of the same issue), we can decide how our perception comes across to each other! We need to start using this forum and concept for all racial incidents.

Eight months after the O.J. incident, I was at an all-black "Town Hall" meeting with the theme "Let's clean up our neighborhoods." In attendance were Cabrini residents, community activists, firemen, press, cops, celebrities, and city officials. Near the end of the night, one man stood up and said something that everyone was in agreement with, though it had nothing to do with the meeting.

"It's been a little while now, and, um, well, some of my best friends are white, and I don't know, but O.J. messed it up for a lot of good people...I just wish a lot of whites would let go of how they think we feel about the whole situation."

(YOU SEE ME, BUT DO YOU SEE ME?)

On Labor Day of 1995, Congressman Christopher Shays spent the night in my Cabrini Green apartment. Mr. Shays is from Connecticut; he represents Bridgeport, Norwalk, and Stamford. He was in Chicago for a meeting on welfare reform that was being held the next day, and he wanted to experience firsthand a project community. He even told his personal security to leave. "It makes no sense that the housing projects are being handled by HUD instead of the city," he stated while walking through the neighborhood.

One of my friends, KRAZE, and I took Mr. Shays (whom I shall refer to as Christopher) on a personal tour of the area, showing him firsthand what he'd heard so much about. "If I would have gone on a regular CHA tour," he said, "it would have been impersonal and boring, but now I can see things for what they truly are. Thank you."

As we walked around the hood, people stopped to talk with him, giving suggestions and complaints about Cabrini's present stage and future. But one thing stuck in Christopher's mind, which he continued to mention, and after he repeated it, I also pondered the observation. He noticed that even though it was late (about midnight), young children sat outside unattended by their parents. And though this had become familiar to my eyes over the years, I painfully agreed.

Being with Christopher was a somewhat helpful wake-up call in my balance.

His short visit reminded me of perceptions that I take for granted because I live in an area that is not the norm, simply the norm to me. A lot of times, we see things but we really don't see them. This is a cousin to "visual effect," because we're looking at something but we're not seeing it for what it is, or if we do, we do nothing about it.

There have been times when living in Cabrini has been hard on my soul. How do I become a community leader without appearing to be a superhero? How do I make a change without losing the essence of Cabrini that makes it Cabrini? How do I get drug dealers to stop selling drugs when people won't hire them? How do I get people to hire them? How do I get kids to stop hanging out all night, when their parents are hanging out all night, and getting drugs from the drug dealers who can't get a job?

So my question to Cabrini is, you see me, but do you see me?

Christopher Shays' actions spoke for themselves. Coming to Cabrini Green by himself, with no involvement of the news and media during his stay, walking through the neighborhood to openly talk with residents, and in the end spending the night with (at the time) a complete stranger…I will say, I was impressed.

We sat up later than planned, but as I went to bed I couldn't help but feel that some solid questions had been answered for Christopher. Upon leaving, he woke me, thanked me, and then walked himself out. I watched his departure from my window to make sure he hadn't forgotten which way to go, which he hadn't.

Christopher wrote me a nice thank-you letter a couple of weeks later and insisted that I look him up whenever in D.C. It's fair to say that we live two different lifestyles. Christopher saw me for me, because he wanted to see who I was. He made an effort, as minute as it may have been for a night, to make sure his visual effect had substance. If it takes going out of your way momentarily to educate yourself, then that's what is needed.

Don't let your visual effect hamper your education or your life.

(WHOSE SIDE?)

When I was in high school, a friend of mine, Alonzo, came to me with a problem. Alonzo (who was black) was the star running back of our football team. He'd been caught cheating by his girlfriend, Shante, and she had left him for a white track star at our school named Rick. Although Alonzo was hurt, I convinced him that if it was meant to be, they'd be back together soon enough. However, that lasted only two weeks, because Alonzo was being teased by Shante's friends that Rick was a better person, friend, and lover, until he was so upset and humiliated that he could take no more.

Alonzo went looking for Rick during lunch break and found him. Outside, a large crowd gathered, as Alonzo made it apparent that Rick would have to fight. Though Rick was caught off guard by Alonzo's sudden rage, he realized that the fight was inevitable. They fought until they both were tired, and I saw something interesting happen.

All of Rick's black friends who were there with him started siding with and moving around to Alonzo's side, cheering Alonzo on. All of Alonzo's white friends started moving toward Rick's side, cheering him on. In fact, the whole crowd seemed split in two! They fought until both guys were so tired of slugging each other that they looked foolish. Seeing that it was a tie, I then pushed my way through the crowd to break it up, as they both held on to each other. They were literally holding each other up! Nothing was accomplished, and as everyone looked around and realized how foolish they too looked, they went back to the sides they had been on at first.

As soon as races argue or there's a confrontation, we immediately look at race instead of what's right and wrong. This is a visual effect we have to diminish, because its intellectual perception is prehistoric, thus crippling our morals. How the hell can we get ahead as a nation if we feel it's morally right to cheer for the negative factor (the negative factor being whatever we relate to)? Our visual effect is just that.

Three months later, Rick and Alonzo became good friends.

(WITHIN A SECOND)

Our eyes are windows, and though they are connected to the outer world of reality, it is our brains that decipher the light vibrations of this outer reality, compute this data into meaning, and then file it. So our brain, in actuality, is true sight. All this happens in milliseconds. Our perception is connected to our past experiences, feeding us data, which in turn is connected to emotions. Within seconds, our minds compute what we recognize as perception and thus **create** the emotions. Do you understand the significance? I said **create** the emotions—which means, you are basically and literally your worst enemy at all times of the day, because everything that you absorb, filter, and process is connected to your emotional response—which you've created, and is how you perceive and react, as well as how others perceive and react to you. So the next portion, "Racial Perception," shows you at a glance how your mathematical input computes.

(Racial Perception line)
-10 -9 -8 -7 -6 -5 -4 -3 -2 -1—0 +1 +2 +3 +4 +5 +6 +7 +8 +9 +10

Let us view this negative-positive racial line. Let us generalize here. All the negative numbers simply represent bad experiences we've personally had with other races. Too, we cannot forget hearsay (mostly stereotyping), which, depending on how negatively it is perceived (even if one incident is factual), adds to the boosting of negative numbers.

For example: You are a white woman coming home from work. Last month, a black male was caught in the act of trying to rape a white woman in the alley, two blocks from your apartment. This act registers as a negative seven (-7) in your mind, but has been boosted up to a negative nine (-9) because of the media's showing it over and over for three weeks straight. However, what was left out of the reported incident after the first two days was that the police officer who stopped the attempted rape was black! Furthermore, the black officer lives at the mouth of the alley—the first house! Which only registers as a positive five (+5) in your mind. Negative nine, minus positive five, leaves negative four. The negative four is the determining factor, and the influence you abide by, so you cross the street. You do this every time you get near the alley, and have been doing so for the last three weeks! And this is what literally happens in your brain, to everyone. We compute. Mathematics truly is a universal concept in all that we do, perceive, and influence.

You are a young black teen living in the projects. You have a choice in going to school—either through rough gang-infested blocks, or through a rich white neighborhood. The rich white neighborhood registers as a negative six (-6) in your mind, because of the way the white people look at you, as well as because the police sometimes pull over to ask why you are in that area. However, the gang-infested blocks register a negative eight (-8) because of the physical threat! You've been chased and had to run for your life. Negative eight, minus negative six, leaves negative two. Though both are negatives, the lesser of the two becomes the dominant influence, and hence, you speedily walk through the rich white neighborhood.

You are an elderly white male at the airport, getting your luggage. Three young men approach you wanting to carry your luggage and put you in a cab. One of the men is Hispanic, one white, and one black. Instantly, you remember last week and the white male who helped you. He dropped the bags, took his time, and had his hand out for a tip; this is a negative four (-4). As you look at the black male, you instantly think about the black man who left your daughter with two kids and is nowhere to be found; this is a negative seven (-7). You quickly glance at the Hispanic man, who reminds you of your mailman and you think of how reliable he is; this automatically registers as a positive four (+4). Negative seven, minus negative four, leaves negative three. So, the white male's influence on you is not as negative as the black male's. However, the positive four that is registered by the Hispanic male obviously dominates and dismisses the other two. You hand the Hispanic man your luggage.

Our minds **create** racial perception lines instantly, every day, without realizing the mechanics behind it. Don't let preconceived notions, stereotyping, or bad experiences alter or cloud your racial judgments. All races do this. Pay attention.

(DARK vs. LIGHT)

There are waves of change that affect black relationships in the ghetto every five to seven years. Presently, blacks share a society with whites as Americans, but blacks have their own, invisible, minor sub-society perks within their own diversity, which often can be damaging to themselves— complexion being one. There will be years when dark-skinned men will be **in**, by white America as well. And then it will slowly play out, and light-skinned black men will be **in**, and again, whites will be swayed by the immediate commercial preference. The diversity continues because not only do they have a societal preference, but a personal one. Dark-skinned or brown-skinned women are attracted to light-skinned men, and light-skinned women prefer dark-skinned men. Although you may see dark-skinned couples or light-skinned couples, it's not too often (and will vary through the years). What's more ironic is that when you cross the racial barrier, it often doesn't matter. For instance, a light-skinned black woman may not be attracted to a light-skinned black male; however, she will be interested in a white male.

What whites don't know is that this influence within black ghetto culture pushes and discriminates the visual perception level to the utmost. In fact, it is even and often not dared to be mentioned by blacks themselves! How tragic can it be that **complexion** determines outlook, preference, prestige, and sometimes violence?

Okay, this stems from the time of slavery because, as we know, Africans are dark complected, and the skin tone (due to melanin) is not as variegated as in African Americans. So obviously, the contrast from dark to light (**blue-black** to **redbone**, as we call it) came from interbreeding with other races: Indian, white, Hispanic, etc., whether by force or by choice, which was often critical (back then) because the lighter you were determined better avenues. The concept of being **lighter** stuck with blacks, as being more qualified for whatever reason, for jobs, marriage, acceptance—or let's just say society. It was a break from the norm—you were not as dark as everyone else. You were special. Many great-grandmothers, even grandmothers, still feel the same way to this day, favoring the light-skinned grandkids over the dark ones. This obviously causes resentment in the dark-skinned boys toward the light ones, and this has trickled down through the years, even though black society hides its discrepancies.

With the streets being more hardcore, it's easier for resentment to come out! Thus, it does. Dark-skinned brothers feel more buck wild, game knowledgeable, and qualified (in their minds) to be on the streets than the light-skinned brothers, often viewing the light-skinned brothers as being pretty boys and/or relating them to more job opportunities, blending in better, gaining society's acceptance, and crossing over more successfully with other races, especially women. This causes a resentful, violent overtone, because the mindset is that they (the dark-skinned brothers) have nothing to lose; they are the bottom of the barrel in the contrast of white to black, with white being the top of society's bracket. (Another quick insight into the mindset is that any type of scratch or mark on the skin is visible in light-skinned men, whereas a black eye or a red mark on a dark-skinned guy is not as visible. So, if a light-skinned brotha had a fight with a dark-skinned brotha and beat him up, the damage is not as visible as it would be on a light-skinned brotha, which continues the false mindset that the darker you are, the more hardcore you are.) This often causes an instant negative perception by view alone (on the streets) of light-skinned men by dark-skinned men—which is ridiculous, and is discrimination in itself within the black urban community. Too, it's important to add that Hollywood (black movies) has helped by depicting the villain in movie after movie as dark-skinned, which continues mass idealism in the negative dark-skinned perception.

Visual effects don't stop with the black male. Black women, too, have their visual mishaps and altercations. Light-skinned women, often called **redbones**, are hated (on the street level) by dark-skinned and brown-skinned women. Much of this is due to the favoritism shown to redbones through music (lyrics), music videos, movies and basically the ideology that black men (even society) perceive toward minority beauty; the lighter you are the more pretty and sexy you appear to be.

Wow, such a diverse racial concept. We have come such a long way, and yet we struggle with so many diversities within our present culture. Visual effects are as big as society makes them. Don't be a follower; be a leader.

DRUGS

Slamming the phone down, Kevin, a forty-five–year-old black male from Chicago's South Side yelled, "I gave my wife an ultimatum!" Out of breath, he turned to me, flopped down on my couch, and continued, "You either leave that stuff alone, or I'm not coming home!" Though I'd just heard him tell her that, I listened to him about her drug problem that was ruining their marriage.

Approximately 90 percent of U.S.-bound South American cocaine and a massive quantity of heroin transit the region as a whole, mostly over maritime trafficking routes. So let's just be honest; this multibillion-dollar industry is affecting America, and it is getting worse! Ya think?

As cocaine became more prevalent in America, the price on the street sales dropped dramatically. When this happened, it became accessible in the ghetto. "Cocaine used to be a rich man's habit and a poor man's dream," said Willie, a fifty-six-year-old black construction worker from Manhattan.

In 1983, crack cocaine hit the streets of New York. This was precooked cocaine, so you could smoke it immediately after purchasing it. Before that, it was sold in powder form for snorting, and had to be cooked in order to be smoked. The price also dropped, from a hundred dollars a pack (and up) to fifty, to twenty-five, to ten, and now to five dollars. There are often **two-dollar spots**, where you can purchase a crack hit for two bucks, but they never last long.

By 1987, as the price dropped more and more, upper-class and middle-class blacks spread the word of the immense new pleasure that cocaine had to offer, and since it was accessible on the streets (and easy to get), it become a hobby. Yes, this new killer, this poison, this street cancer was being flirted with by those in and around the ghetto. Why?! Because no one knew at that point in time what would happen down the line. No one knew the grave injustice it would bring to the ghetto! (Except **the powers that be.**)

Kevin picked up my phone to call her back, but she wasn't there. He tried two more times with no luck. "I bet you any money she's out there chasing that shit!" he yelled. "She couldn't even wait to see if I was gonna come home!"

Now that blacks and minorities could get their hands on larger quantities of cocaine, there had to be ways it could become easily accessible to the ghetto without the middlemen—middlemen being the ones who knew the cocaine dealers outside the ghetto, who trusted only them to bring in those sales. However, this person (the middleman) would be eliminated, because of the drop in price, now bringing distribution to the ghetto, from within the ghetto, this being made possible by those with money in the ghetto that bought the large quantities of cocaine (because of it being cheaper) could now employ workers. Overnight, this became a business. Remember, too, that drugs and illegal police doings have been in the ghetto for decades, but with crack hitting the scene at this new, ridiculously low price, along came havoc.

At first, when crack hit the ghetto (as far as widespread sales distribution), it was sold from crack houses. At that point in time, selling crack cocaine on the streets was still too risky. The police had heard about crack and were expecting to find it on people in the streets, so they started frisking people at will. This was the beginning of a whole new police ethic consisting of illegal searches, force, and brutality, which came about when cocaine became more rampant in the ghetto.

Crack houses sprouted overnight. Bars and gates were put up on these houses and workers had shifts for this twenty-four-hours-a-day, seven-days-a-week operation. At first, everyone had someone they were working for who put them on salary (usually weekly), sometimes by the pack and how much you sold. But as time went on, three things happened. The first was that competition became fierce. The second was that competition became fiercer! Crack houses were going up everywhere, prices were dropping, and other competitors' bags were bigger. Third, violence suddenly came with the territory. Shootouts over drug turf exploded, and suddenly everyone was against each other. At first, if drug dealers found out that their customers were going elsewhere, they'd try to beat up the customers, as if they had been unfaithful, and then go after the rival dealers for snatching their customers.

With all this madness came more trickery. People were now cutting off customers at the bypass—meaning, if your crack house was in the middle of the block, someone would be waiting outside (a few houses down) to steal your customers before they got there, which opened the door for more flamboyant shysterism.

***

(Faith in Mr. Hole)

During this time period, there was a powerful entity that the younger generation will not remember (you'd have to be old school). We called it Mr. Hole. This was a crack house that, instead of bars and gates, had a small hole in the door. This small hole was the beginning and end, or the end and beginning, of your destiny. This little hole was the equivalent of shooting dice. Did you feel lucky? Well, did you, punk? Because, for a dope fiend (heroin addict), going to this hole with his last ten bucks that he'd worked hard for was truly a painful gamble! Your whole soul and being was enticed by this hole, because sometimes you'd put your money in and get something out—and sometimes you wouldn't. The difference between the hole and the bars was that it gave the workers (those selling the drugs) the opportunity to make a little extra money—meaning, since the customer couldn't see you through the door (no bars or gates), he couldn't point you out once you took his money. The **Big Man** (the one who ran the drug house) only came by to drop off drugs—and only stayed for a hot moment—which made it hard for you to catch him in order to tell him, so as to get your money back. And you knew that you wouldn't, because it was basically your word against theirs since you couldn't see anyone! You were basically out your money. This is what made the hole so detrimental: It became God to you, fate, even equal to life. And you hated it. You hated it. And yet, you devilishly loved it.

I remember one time, while selling out of the hole, a brotha I knew quite well came to shop. I had served a lady, and heard him ask her, "How is it today, boo, they treating us right?" She replied, "Shit, I'm cool, I don't know about you!" And that was enough for him to have faith in Mr. Hole. He knocked on the door, and I replied, "What's up?" He responded, "One time," while sticking his ten bucks through the hole. I took the ten bucks and went to sit on the couch by the door. Although I knew him, I was thirsty to make some extra money. Screw him; it was his turn to be the victim! This was the beginning of the end for him. That man literally waited four hours! During those four hours by the door, he cried, sang songs, talked to the hole, and tried to persuade other customers not to shop. I wanted to go out there and crack his head open, down to the white meat, but knew that I couldn't because I was the only one working the spot, and I felt petty for snatching his ten bucks, only to lose over four hundred because of him (he had made me miss over 40 customers!) I was young.

Mr. Hole didn't last too long, little over a year. There were just too many problems with its instability: crackheads got fed up, cops were called, and workers got pettier. To this day, crackheads who remember will tell you that Mr. Hole was God and Satan all in one.

***

Since crack houses were getting raided, families were getting evicted, and customers were being stolen, it was only natural and a matter of time before crack and heroin were taken outside to the actual streets. As more people went outside to set up shop, crack houses became extinct; only being used to smoke out of, no selling. More people were now selling cocaine for themselves, and less for a "boss figure," so to speak. When this happened, since the operation moved outside a form of security was needed for safety—not just from the police, but from customers who might pose a threat, possibly stickup artists. Now, here in Chicago, as well as in Los Angeles, the street organizations (or gangs, if you will) have always implemented and run the drug scene, as far as the streets were concerned. New York is similar, but there are more gangs, so there are more crews and locations (such as projects and block areas) where those in your area with juice are supplying the weight. So security in your area, and deciding on how your group puts it together, is mandatory. It basically ensures your safety.

"One day a few years back, she sold her wedding ring to a damn dealer for three dime bags! I had to go find him and buy it back for two hundred dollars!" sobbed Kevin.

From the beginning of the '80s to now, an entire generation has died within. (Meaning, the first consumers in the ghetto that got hooked on drugs when they lowered the price, had become zombies and now in rehab.) Those who first started selling cocaine and Karachi (synthetic heroin) in "pony packs" (the paper that packaged both crack and Karachi had a horse emblem on the outside) have ruined their lives with indulgence. They're simply strung out, and their children are now paying for it by selling. Of the urban youth that sell drugs, 82 percent have parents who use drugs. It has become a way of life. The domino effect has struck, and it has struck hard. For example, in the early '80s, as disco died, Reaganomics clamored the ghetto, and jobs for minorities seemed routinely fewer, many who had no education or job experience felt helpless. Minorities realized that not everyone could be this superfly stereotype that the '70s had created—it took money! And then WHAM! The crazy '80s, which seemed to start off completely white-collar, offered a way out. Here was an escape—and not only that, but you could get paid for it. So at this time, though many people selling cocaine did not actually smoke it, they did snort it, and it was only a matter of time. Too, since all the first crack houses were places where the residents indulged, how could someone, day in and day out, sell from that house with all those indulging and all that smoke wafting around (not knowing how powerful secondhand smoke is) without sooner or later wanting to try it? And remember, the first women who indulged were healthy and fit before they started going downhill, so what better way to get a free high than to throw your body at the workers? Once you gave them the sex, you could eventually persuade them to indulge, which is what happened. Seventy percent of workers who were first put in dope houses were turned out by the women who were the owners of the house, and their company. As the domino effect trickles down, we still have to remember a key factor I mentioned earlier. Since the price had dropped, now making it accessible to the hood, this new product (as it was thought to be) had no futuristic damages yet! No one knew what was to come—the aftereffect. And I don't mean instantly after; I'm talking about weeks, that turned into torturous months, and finally into agonizing years. What hell.

The first thing that hit the community was the urge for more! The demand for more cocaine (once the price dropped) was unreal. There simply could not be enough for the ghetto. Crack houses sold out daily, and customers were told to wait or come back periodically. Then, as soon as the money was spent, the dilemmas started. At first, for weeks the customer marveled at this new high that was like no other; so intense, so different, so uninhibited—and so costly, as bank accounts diminished.

But as money began to wither, so did morals. Women who never would have sold their bodies did. People lost weight, stole, and pawned valuables. (The ghetto was already poor and unsafe, but now, with this new factor that had escalated the unsafe element toward what appeared to be a frenzy, crime naturally rose).

"When she started losing weight, she said it was depression. I cried one night because I noticed my son's TV gone, but I was too scared to ask her where it was because I already knew the answer...That's when I knew I had lost her," stated Kevin.

Times thus far were good for the seller, but he too would be damaged. At first, "credit" was valued. People with reliable jobs were trusted with extras until payday. But this was simply because in the beginning, all customers were known practically on a first-name basis, due to the carefulness of how you sold, and who you sold to. But as a cutthroat mentality set in, along with so many other crack houses, people didn't pay their debts—and why should they, when they could go down the street for the same thing and spend more money? Then workers (because of under-the-table indulging) started coming up short on packs and money. So, workers weren't to be trusted, customers now couldn't be trusted, and the strain grew on the initial supplier, "The Boss Man." Taking losses is part of the drug game, but with cocaine now on the streets and still a fresh avenue with so much competition, stickups, and police busts, one couldn't afford losses, but they happened. And though many realized the drug game was too much to handle (harder than they thought at first) and collapsed, three new opponents opened up shop just as quickly. The game was cold, but it was fair.

The ghetto had now built a whole following revolving around cocaine and heroin. Then began an era of self-mutilation, which began to spread. You see, the problem with the ghetto is that it's a trendsetter, without even knowing it—meaning that, although it may get the initial ideas from elsewhere, they are absorbed and literally recreated in its own version or style. This has happened with clothes, dances, stores, food, and styles; this too happened with cocaine. Upper-class whites had the money and the luxury of using cocaine as a leisure drug. But as it hit the ghetto, the land of the poor, who hustled and worked hard to get that twenty-dollar bag or that ten-dollar rock—those people savored every bit of it, because nine times out of ten, it was their last little bit of change.

If a white businessman dropped a crumb onto his carpet, missing his pipe, it was left there (he need not bother to look for it). However, if a black brother from the ghetto dropped his crumb, missing his antenna (Freeze! Don't nobody move!), he was on his hands and knees searching the floor—because he wasn't going to waste that shit! And you see, along with cocaine in the ghetto came all the accoutrements: homemade pipes out of actual household pipes, television antennas, car antennas, aluminum foil man pipes, soda cans, and the damn cardboard inside a roll of toilet tissue.

Immediately, words (or nicknames) had to be created for these people who smoked crack because their actions became too noticeable. First came "base heads," then later "cluckers," "dope fiends," and today "hypes." The actions of people who use heavy cocaine are worldwide. The awkwardness of swaying and moving jerkily, with loose coordination, is a prime example. Also noticeable is not being able to stand up straight, with good posture, for a period of time

"I came home early one day and the house smelled terrible. I walked in the kitchen and my wife was on the floor, passed out. I cleaned up her mess, threw her pipe away, and called rehab," whispered Kevin.

So, by the time these crack houses took it to the streets, crack babies had already been conceived. The following year they were born, and today they are now selling cocaine to their indulging parents. Here's the literal domino effect to recap: The price was dropped so that those in the ghetto could profit, indulge, and distribute. Workers in the crack houses started closet smoking, not realizing at that point the consequences ("Don't get high off your own supply" seemed too corny a phrase to grasp) because of its newness to the scene. It was taken to the streets, and by that time the damage had been done. Along with this new concept came violence, separation, and eventually despair. Children were born into the lives of base heads unable to support them. Morals vanished, along with self-esteem. The crack babies grew up seeing what they did not want to become—their parents. So their conscience had no remorse for selling drugs because their parents were on drugs and had been taken away.

By 1990, selling cocaine, heroin, and weed became an actual job and a support system in the ghetto. To this day, many whites still truly don't understand the depth of selling narcotics in the ghetto; what it means and how it's perceived. Basically, it's looked at as being an alternative job, and although this can't be conceived by whites, it is simply the truth. Whites only look at the right/wrong issue, because their immediate society only allows that much leverage. Either you're doing right or you're doing wrong, either you're abiding by the law or you're breaking the law—there's no in-between. And I'm not here to justify selling drugs (in fact, I wish we could eliminate drug trafficking in America); I'm here to discuss the facts for understanding and therefore addressing the problem. And our goal should be the same—to see what solutions are available. Although drugs are rampant in the ghetto, they are everywhere in America and getting worse—much worse.

Kids in the ghetto grow up faster than kids in mainstream society—meaning, having to deal with the struggles of life at an earlier age; babysitting themselves; a lack of monitoring; having to clothe themselves; developing their own eating habits, etc. There's an immediate need for money that their parents can't meet. Which of course means there's no family structure, no transportation, cheap clothes—and who the hell wants to go to school looking tacky, with no pocket money (let alone an allowance). Thus, the dropout rate increases. Who's going to hire you? You can't even get your baby some Pampers! Yes, your little daughter—which Keisha had by you in your sophomore year because she was the only one who cared about you, but she finally left you because you didn't have anything! And you know in your heart that a lot of guys in the neighborhood have slept with your mama because she's on that shit, and you also know that these same guys talk about you because you dress like a damn bum! This is how it happens. And it's easy for us to stand on the outside saying how we would have stayed in school and done the right thing, but that's our problem. Our biggest fault as Americans is to criticize one another. Instead of closing our eyes and actually thinking about being in someone else's predicament, someone else's world and surroundings, we immediately shun them, instantly blocking the understanding. It's all too easy.

As I looked at Kevin, I saw the pain from the loss of a marriage. He sat there speechless for twenty minutes, and then finally spoke. "She stayed in rehab for three weeks, and broke out to buy another pipe...She just wasn't ready."

So, you have no money, and Lonnie and the guys keep asking you to join the team. As bad as you want to, and as bad as you need to (you keep telling yourself), you decline—many times. But you know you can't get a job and you realize that you need money, now. Right now! Lonnie and the guys dress well, have transportation, don't indulge, take care of their children, and keep money in their pockets. So you join. Thus starts the cycle,

But with this new generation, standards have been gradually set. For instance, seeing that their parents have nothing and having their parents stripped from them, their sense of the power of this poison is strong! This new generation (90 percent) will not indulge. This new generation also has learned to save and manage money. In fact, this new generation has become more business-oriented than we thought. Think about it. Their whole world has been poured into this way of living. These young adults have conjured a set structure around their own business; those more determined, knowledgeable, creative, and business-wise make it further up the ladder than those just seeking enough to make it from week to week, as in the working world. These individuals have learned business tactics, such as sales of a commodity, packaging and visual appeal, profit sharing, mathematics and accounting, wholesale, bargaining, customer service, competition, promotion and advertisement, standard security, chemistry, timing and patience, savings and loans, distribution, and financial security. Bear in mind that all of this is just at the street level.

I realize that these skills may sound overrated to those who still may not understand the street pharmaceutical policies, so let us examine them further. Your financial and bargaining tactics immediately have to be put to use when purchasing your weight (bulk quantity of cocaine or heroin), because you're going to your supplier with a certain amount of money and want the most and best quality for it. You have to get your supplier to realize that there are other possibilities for you, since so many other people are selling weight. Your goal is to get him to offer you at the best deal possible, because he'll want to keep you as a client, always getting more from and spending more with him. Then it's off to the laboratory, where your chemistry and pharmaceutical talents pay off. Most cocaine when sold in weight comes in powder form, which you as the seller will have to rock up (make into crack form). There's no need to discuss this detailed chemistry process because it's not important, but all chemists have their own techniques which determine how strong or weak their product will be, and shows how good they are in the laboratory.

With heroin, your skills lie in the mixing of the product and how potent you make it. This process is called "stepping on." What you're doing is taking whatever product you decide to mix and cut it with (again, the specific substances are not important) to stretch the heroin (increasing the amount, which allows you to make more money). The problem is that the more you step on it, the less potent it is, which sends your customers elsewhere.

Now to your packaging, timing, and patience, because at this point packaging can take tireless patience with hours of agonizing work. Some people do this alone, while others enjoy the company of those they trust (usually these people have invested their money and are on the team). You're taking large quantities of a substance and breaking it into portions, with each bag accurate to its financial value. This is much harder than it sounds, takes hours to finish, and requires skill, accuracy, and determination. Then, in order for you to sell the product, little techniques that differentiate you from your competitors are important. One part of this would be visual appeal. The bags containing your substance must be representative of your statement about your product. For instance, all drug sellers usually create a name for their product so that the word can spread (this being part of your promotion and advertising). If you label your product Red Dragon, you would sell it in bright red bags or bags with a red dragon on them. A Green Hornet label would require green bags or bags with a hornet or bee on them. In New York, it was mostly vials instead of bags; these vials had different colored tops, so there were still names for the product.

Once you were finished "bagging up" (packaging) your product, it was mathematics that took over. Everything was to be registered, accounted for, and figured into profit. This was to see where you stood, how much you'd be gaining, and how much extras you could spend before breaking even. Since competition is fierce, you'd sacrifice a little money by making your bags bigger than average, to keep your current customers and make new ones. The entire process of chemistry, chopping, mixing, and bagging up is physically and mentally exhausting, but your job is far from over. Because now you're to the hustling stage, which involves customer service, bargaining, sales and distribution, and a hell of a mouth piece. Many people at this point are usually tired, yet eager to make money.

"I came in one day and found my wife and son arguing, but when they saw me they got quiet. My son finally came to me later and said that his mother had stolen from him, but he wouldn't tell me what. This is when it dawned on me that our fourteen-year-old was selling drugs!" Kevin stated.

"Hustling" is a word that differs between blacks and whites. Many whites (especially older whites) hear the word "hustling" and immediately an act of swindling comes to mind. It's a negative word that relates to someone hustling someone else out of something; or getting over on someone else. However, the word "hustling" to blacks is a positive word, with an entirely different meaning. In basketball, your coach blows his whistle and hollers, "C'mon, get on that hustle! C'mon, pick up your hustle, guys!" This sums it up, because hustling is all about moving and generating the energy and drive you need to get what you want; meaning, through actions and speech, your body becomes a tool for results. And this is what a hustler does in the drug game.

When these young hustlers hit the streets, they already have their location picked out. Customers are coming, and it's time for customer service and sales bargaining. As I said, hustling is all about drive, and this is where you go into action, because the competition surrounds you. Nowadays, wherever street youth sell their drugs, not only is the competition down the street or in the next building (if you're in the projects), but nine times out of ten, it is right there shoulder to shoulder with them (let alone those on their same team), all manipulating the customer to buy their product. Though there may be a code of taking turns on this particular block, it doesn't stop the true hustler from advertising his merchandise. The usual code is, if a customer doesn't come up and ask for a particular name such as Red Dragon, then it's an open market and whoever had the last sale it's on the next person in line; basically taking turns (all according to who got on the dope spot first, second, etc). But if the customer comes and asks for it by name, then you have the right to be the only one to sell your product. However, if rules have been set that it's an open market (and no one is honoring turns), then hustlers show their skills, constantly outdoing the next man.

For instance, a customer walks up. Everyone surrounds the customer, with their hands out showing their product. "I know you heard of Red Dragon, sweetheart. C'mon and get it because I'm almost out! It's going like water, baby!" Another guy cuts in: "You don't want those little pebbles, baby. This is my second batch; I sold out an hour ago and—" He gets cut off by another guy, who's had a good day and can afford a little loss just to get her five bucks, but more importantly, so she'll come back and spread the word. He hollers over the crowd, "Excuse me! Sweetheart, you seen the rest, now get with the best. I got two for five right here!" And he gets the sale. This hustling technique comes on all different angles, and if he wants a solid customer that will definitely come back looking for him, he continues (as she's walking away, pleased that she got two for the price of one), "Hey, Boo! Come back for a minute, today is your lucky day...here," and hands her another bag. "Just remember Green Hornet, baby, and don't ask for nothing else. I'll make sure you get treated right." By now she's overwhelmed and will remember this day for a long time—a devoted customer. Customers come every two to three minutes and often a herd will come all at once, where everyone will get a turn, regardless of the size of their rocks, because the customers just want to get their stuff and get the hell outta there. An hour later, a stickup man attempts to rob the spot, but he's beaten down by security, his gun is taken, and he's thrown in the alley. The following hour security yells, "Get little!" which is the code for "the police are headed straight for you," so everyone breaks out, to get away. Those who get away check their sales and commodity at home to see how they did for the day. Money is put to the side for financial security (just in case something goes wrong and bond is needed), and later that night or early in the morning, you're back on the set, eager to finish and start all over again.

"My son and my wife started coming in the house around the same time, late at night. It got to the point that I couldn't and wouldn't have sex with her. I just didn't want to, she wasn't the same person anymore. I had lost my household and my family," mourned Kevin.

Though there's more detail in this, I just wanted to give a generalization of the real world these young adults live in. I've often talked to, even interviewed, many of these young men (and women) and a recurring comment they all have made is that they would love to get out of the drug game, if they just had a realistic outlet. When you don't have a job and you're trying to survive in a society that has a cutthroat mentality about right and wrong, your perception of legal work can't possibly be the same as mainstream. However, everything else can! These young men hate what they do, but are good at it because they have to be in order to literally keep their heads above water due to a lack of parenting. Remember, in the beginning (twenty-three years ago), this new drug market was fresh and untapped. But as you can see, the present day scenario entails polished business tactics that have accumulated over time and are now quite different than what their parents went through. However, one thing did happen that adds to the seriousness of the whole matter. Each year (in the ghetto), the drug dealers got younger and younger, and sadly have now been factually registered between the ages of twelve and nineteen. Most of those twenty and up have been registered as selling weight. Since the age has dropped because of the dependency on money at an early age, so has the trust in the police for these kids. How can these youth trust the police, if they're taught to run from them so they won't get put in the Audi home (county jail for minors) or county? It's survival, and though it seems tragic, it's real. And instead of pointing fingers at those we feel are responsible (because it's too late for that), we need to look at solutions.

***

(ARE YOU READY?)

It used to amaze me how people, places, and things entered into my life! Now, I simply appreciate the newness, because nothing in this world happens by accident.

In training to become a Substance Abuse Counselor (yes, all those years of selling drugs, and now I'm trying to help people get off 'em—go figure), I have run into so many recovering addicts. Some I know, some I don't, some I used to serve, some my friends used to serve, some used to serve themselves and fell off, but now miraculously they are staying clean and have changed their lives. So what was it? What on earth could have helped these people who were once thought of as lost souls?

The three factors:

1. People have to submit to the fact that they have a problem (this is easier said than done) and **want** to seek help. They must now search for the solution and aid in recovery.

2. Support Groups—vital because it's pertinent that drug addicts create longevity in sobriety, thus the support groups (often considered home base's) become essential and often mandatory.

3. Sponsorship. Once on the Twelve Step program you will seek a **Sponsor.** The relationship between you and your **Sponsor** is quite personal. A **Sponsor** is someone who aids along your recovery in maintaining sobriety.

So where do these support groups come from? What are they? I'm sure everyone is familiar with AA (Alcoholics Anonymous), NA (Narcotics Anonymous), and CA (Cocaine Anonymous). There are many more, but these are the main three drug-related support groups.

I walked into a meeting one day and was blown away! If you've never been to a meeting—go to one! Even if you don't get high. This support system is better than church. It is testimony, counseling, therapy, struggle, and family (regardless of race) all in one. Really. I used to see people on TV shows or movies that would end up in treatment or at a meeting, and I used to think, how cheesy! All the meetings looked boring, and it put me in the frame of mind that these people were losers in life; they couldn't cut it; they were stuck in that place—either being made to go, or going to please someone else. How wrong I was!

Man, sometimes meetings are off the chain! Sometimes they are quiet and deep. Regardless, they work! And you can go across America and find meetings everywhere, in each city, town, and district! From basements to churches, from storefronts to people's homes, they are everywhere—and I never knew how big it was or how organized—really. From young teens to elders, everyone is there to support the cause and all have a common goal—to stay clean.

With a Sponsor, sky's the limit. You get to pick who you would like to be your Sponsor; and you exchange numbers. All Sponsor's have a Sponsor, as do they and so on. The job of a Sponsor is to help you along the twelve steps, keep you focused and assure you (as long as it may take) that there is meaningful life outside the drug arena.

Deemed the grandfather of all programs (as well as the Prince of Twelfth Steppers), **Dr. Bob** took his last drink on June 10, 1935, which is considered to be the founding date of Alcoholics Anonymous. In 1939, the *Big Book* was written by Dr. Bob and his partner, Bill Wilson, along with other early members, and is somewhat the bible of sobriety. Eventually came other books for other addictions, with the same goal.

It is important in any gathering or cause to have a unified theme and goal. For an addict to want to become clean is a common tie, but to actually make the change to becoming clean, and staying clean, is a selective duty that needs a support system. All can relate to one another! There are no qualifications to join—other than the will to stay clean. Throughout America, programs have been developed to aid these sobriety endeavors, such as HayMarket Center and Tasc. Cook County Jail has even developed a specialized program entitled Daily Report, which has done wonders for the men while helping them stay clean. Change is needed on the streets.

As I mentioned earlier, it used to amaze me how people, places, and things occurred in my life. While writing this segment, I received a call from a good friend, who sought my assistance in getting her twenty-year-old son serious help. He's an alcoholic and has been a problem in her home, threatening and violent, often throwing things. I gave her the information on HayMarket, she called and set a quick appointment, he's agreed to go, and they are actually out the door in hopes of progress. It won't be easy for him, but he's made the first step, and luckily he has an immediate support system.

Drugs have damaged unborn children, engendered the proliferation of child care facilities, and continue to keep the ghettos just that— crumbling ghettos. If you know anyone on drugs, and you care the least bit about them, get them some help. Often people want to get off drugs, but they just don't know the options available. Go to a meeting.

Are you ready?

***

I have a book coming soon, with one of its key components relating to the entire drug matter, entitled "Solutions." However, my goal in this book is to look at the problems and understand them before we get to the solutions, because many times the solution is in the understanding itself.

We've looked at twenty-three years to see the starting stages, so that we can visualize its gradual evolution to the present day. Twenty years to come, it's inevitable that new drugs will be available. The sad part is that many of these will be legal. Understand that all issues and angles of this street product and culture are growing, and along with that comes the flip side—the need for and use of sellers—but let us not punish the culprit if he's really the victim. Let's work together as a country to stop the domino effect of drugs that he's simply at the end of.

Kevin called three more times, never reaching his wife. He left my house that night, never seeing her again. Two weeks later, she was found dead from an overdose.

SARCASM

I t's important that we look at the difference in culture, so that we can understand culture. Sometimes, it's the little things we take for granted, that we just assume another race is expected to know, let alone our own race. Sarcasm is one that we assume everyone understands. But they don't, nor do they give a damn.

Urban blacks and minorities in America live a literal life, which leaves no room for sarcasm. Just think about it: If your everyday life consists of struggle, things are serious and you don't have the leisure time to joke around (especially through sarcastic babble). You're prone to look at life for what it is, simply a day-to-day struggle.

Let's try and define sarcasm. The *Oxford American Dictionary* defines it as being "an ironical remark or taunt." However, it's not so much what it is, but when it's used! We as Americans use it constantly, to the point that it has become routine by most in everyday speech. Those with money who have nothing better to do use it casually. It is now cynical; it has now become a battle of the mind to come out with the best and wittiest sarcastic comment possible. What's that shit all about? (To say something, but to mean something else!)

Too, since many minorities don't waste their time with sarcasm, much of our worlds separate because it's everywhere. Journalists write sarcastically in the newspaper, it's on TV, in movies, books, and the theater, and on down the line, until those that don't use it all the time seem boring or cold. This is crazy. We have that much spare time to waste such energy?

And believe me, I'm not saying sarcasm doesn't have a place in our society, because I think it does. It's just that we're finally coming to a point of being bilingual with our perception of culture, and this is a good thing. In order for us to carry it a step further, we have to realize that the little things, or what we thought were little, just aren't. They are huge roadblocks in communication.

Remember, just because someone may not appear interested in your skilled sarcasm, doesn't seem to catch on, or not as skilled in his attempt to use it, simply means he focuses his energy elsewhere. Get literal sometimes, cut through the attempt to have underlying meanings. You will be perceived better by many, and you too will see the flow of the conversation smoothly absorbed and understood, with no guessing.

Sarcasm is a skill predominantly used (in a demeaning way) by upper-class whites, and can be viewed by the rest of society in how whites view hip-hop. Sarcasm is basically a trend, and may or may not last long in an ever-changing literal world. White people! Listen! Don't jump on the bandwagon with a concept that has no simplistic value other than mentally challenging your own humor, because that's all it is. Whether it lasts or not, use it with those who also use it; don't try and spread it around to the rest of America, which doesn't want to be bothered.

Yes, it's that serious, if you only knew.

CHOICES

A few years back, I used to run a newspaper in Cabrini Green. The name of the paper was *Voices of Cabrini,* and we received mail from all over the United States. Although we didn't have a mail commentary section, I would print letters that interested me, from men doing time in the penitentiary to fans of ours in Florida and Canada trying to get a paper like ours for their community.

One short letter that I received, I just had to follow up on, and though I never printed it (because of its nature, depth, and diversity), I will print it now so we can discuss it in full. It deserves individual attention:

Dear Editor,

My mother is black and she had my brother and I when she was 22. When his father (who is black) found out about the pregnancy he split. My father, who is white, knew her, liked her and approached her (while she was pregnant) when he found out the father left. They soon became a couple and five months after my brother was born, I was conceived. So my brother and I are about a year apart. We grew up close, even our parents are close to us, but that's where I draw the line! I get along with my father and some of his family and that's it. I don't feel the need to be down with white people. And my brother looks up to my father as being dad, I'll admit he's done all the father things for him, but can't my brother see that a lot of whites are against us. Plus all whites I've met seem boring, strict, and unfair. I'm not trying to be mean, but when white people approach me trying to be friends, I turn them down. I could never go out with a white woman and though my parents say I'm being unrealistic about my beliefs, I don't give a damn! Who cares what everybody else thinks I've made my mind up to be pro black to the utmost. Even my brother seems to now all of a sudden be against me, but I've made my choice and I deserve to live my life the way I choose!
Sincerely,

It's my damn choice...

Mr. Choice wrote his real name on the outside of the letter, and enclosed was a telephone number. However, I didn't call for a long time. It seemed to me that he'd made up his mind and there was no room for discussion.

But I often thought about Mr. Choice and his decision. And as the months went by, seeing his letter float around my desk (surrounded by a hundred more), I began to realize something. His letter was fairly well written and to the point, and it seemed to be asking more of a question than anything, the more I thought about it. It seemed as if this wasn't the only letter he'd sent out, as if he wasn't sure his choice was really what he wanted, as if he was seeking a response or some type of advice, or he wouldn't have enclosed his number...so I called. In fact, I called eight times before getting in touch with him. Four of the eight times I called, I talked to his brother. We talked for two hours straight one night, and he finally told me that his brother had been in a car accident, but he wasn't sure if he should give me the information on the hospital until he asked his brother first. He told me to call back the next day, which I did, and I was on my way to the hospital.

Mr. Choice, whose real name was Evan, lay in recovery with two casts around his legs. He had multiple scars, burns, and both his eyebrows and hair were singed off. He was well enough to talk, though in great pain. His girlfriend (who was black) was on her way out; she'd spent the night. After she left, I stood there momentarily blank, admiring the get well cards, balloons, and flowers. I've never been one for small talk, but somehow, as I stood there in front of this young man of nineteen who was lucky to be alive, I wasn't sure how to tackle the issue. And then I was saved.

Evan wasted no time calling me closer to him. I sat in the chair his girlfriend had been in, and he began to talk. In fact, he did all the talking. First about the accident, which he admitted was his fault. He'd been drinking and he ran a red light, smashing into the middle of an eighteen-wheeler!

Evan's Celica was totaled and on fire, and he had passed out inside the car from the impact. Flames were everywhere and no one would dare to get close, scared it was going to blow! A punk rocker, who was working as a delivery carrier and driving by on his scooter, pulled over and risked his life saving Evan. Kicking the windows out, he pulled Evan's body from the burning car. The punk rocker waited for the ambulance, made sure Evan was on it, and left, avoiding the media that did the cover story.

Evan looked at me, smiled, and whispered, "Yup, a white guy saved my life." He then went on to express his deep feelings of foolishness for being so negative, so wrong, and so empty, for so long. He felt as if he'd been given a second chance at life, and was truly happy to know that all his parts were still intact, though broken and scared.

Evan made it quite clear that he wanted me to know something before I left. He said it twice, so that I would think about it and understand it. Evan's message was about choice; his choice between two worlds that he felt he had to decide on. "People have the lazy luxury of being one race and have time to focus their attentions on other things," he said. "Whereas, I felt it impossible to be two races, so I banned the other, the less attractive. In doing this, I was walking around mad as hell, because I knew I was running from responsibility." Evan now sees things for what they are, and finally feels blessed to not have to make this choice between races. He now acknowledges both sides willingly and proudly.

Evan and I talked for several hours about his childhood, parents, brother, and future (with him still doing most of the talking, as I listened), until the door opened and a tall white man walked in. Evan's eyes lit up as he saw his father.

I politely excused myself, thanking Evan for the special talk, not considering it an interview because it was much more, and wished him a speedy recovery. Though he and his father asked me to stay, I felt it appropriate for them to be alone.

To this day, Evan still calls me. He is doing well. When I think of Evan, I think of our nation's rebellious teenagers who feel the need to be different. We all have the decision of choice, but as a teenager learning adult issues, we rebel even more against responsibility. The plight Evan once had is not so much a racial issue, as he may have thought, but simply a choice issue, as he later figured out.

Since he first viewed whites as strict or boring, it's quite natural that this wasn't what he wanted to be. But when he realized that you can't view race on what you perceive, but what it is, he made the ultimate choice—to not make a choice.

COPS

Bad Boys, Bad Boys whatcha gonna do, whatcha gonna do when they come for you?
Bad Boys, Bad Boys whatcha gonna do, whatcha gonna do when they come for you?

Theme from COPS television series

This theme song is basically played out, and sadly represents people getting incarcerated as entertainment. Furthermore, it distinctly separates American people into "us" and "them," with the cops supposedly representing "us" and society's bad citizens as "them."

The '90s marked a new obstacle for the American police force. They'd become "questionable" in the public's eyes. Though cops have been linked to certain corruption incidents (as other major organizations have been over the years), the '90s brought a distinct aroma that claimed stench. As the '90s ended, an image had been branded on the white-collar American mind, something that the rest of us had known all along. Police officers had been brutally taking the law into their own hands, and it was evident: videotapes, news coverage, citizens dying, cell phone pics and video, lawsuits, and eye witnesses coming forth all supported this. Too many negative reports, too much publicity, and too many questions were arising. Who were the police answering to? Why were corrupted individuals left on the force? Why wasn't anything being done? And it persisted.

At this point, different organizations, churches, gangs, and the general public came together. Dates to wear all black and march against police brutality spread like wildfire. Protest after protest, meeting after meeting, neighborhoods answered in disgust.

Here in America, there are different levels of police authority and business tactics, with vast divisions of different ethics and duties (more or less all kinds of job descriptions for all kinds of cops, who will be sent from the highway to the projects). We have to focus on who's sent where and what their role "should" be, as opposed to what it is.

Cops who are sent to the suburban areas (keep in mind that they're from and currently live in the suburbs) have an outlook and are trained specifically for that area. So, cops from the suburbs don't get sent to the inner city's ghettos or the projects, which means a different type of cop does.

The officers who are sent to the projects and ghetto areas are men (and women) that feel they have to act a certain way to get results. Much of this chapter could be written bashing them, but as I said, the intent is to factually shed light so that we can understand them.

If you're a cop, in order to go into an untapped, hardcore, high crime rate area (as far as you're concerned), it's only natural that you would have to psych yourself out to be someone you're not, and develop an aggressive front. Before you explore this new beat, the department and your friends have added to your aggressive front by sitting you down and reminding you of the hardcore situations this area has to offer, seemingly trying to lock it into your brain so that you have to act a certain way in order to survive. Though this is done (as far as they're concerned) for your protection, it defeats who you are, your job, and the community's perception of you.

The problem with this front is that it immediately labels a distinction between "us" and "them"—with you and your police force being "us," and the neighborhood and patrol being "them." Thus, the wall is built mentally and by your actions. The "them" notice the wall, too. You get firsthand experience from your partner who has already been down this road. You are groomed, and the outcome is far from what you expected.

White cops that go into a predominantly black neighborhood have to deal with the immediate issue of race relations between black and white. Before you are a cop, you are white, and are looked upon individually by each person and their past experiences with white people. So you, too, become a new experience with all you encounter. Obviously, this is one less problem that black cops have to deal with in a black community, until they too are on a reverse beat.

So instead of focusing on the positive domino effect you can create, which will reflect on you, your colleagues, possibly even your race, with the position you have in the community, you continue with your Gestapo tactics that you and your colleagues feel are sufficient.

You see, the problem with the police is that they're not sent into the community to be a part of the community. Their job is to patrol and monitor the community, dealing with the crime as it occurs and when they're called. This is the only way that they become a part of the community. Understand. So if you're constantly dealing with crime, or the crime of the neighborhood, then you only know the supposed criminals of the neighborhood: the drug dealers, the gang members, the prostitutes, the boosters, etc., until these (because you are constantly dealing with them) seem a representation of the community. In fact, you begin to know these people by their first names, nicknames, and even last names!

As your dealings with these people increase (as time goes on), you get worse. Your attitude toward "them" is one of superiority. You jump out of your car when approaching a scene, which immediately separates "us" and "them" even more, by your eagerness to approach, rippling their first impression of you. You grab "them" and tell "them" to put their hands on the hood of your car, you illegally search "them" while making sarcastic comments and hoping to find contraband, you watch as your friends smack "them" around while trying to get information, and you sometimes join in to get a taste of the action. Though you may go home at first, uncertain of your hectic day, you con yourself into believing that this is necessary in order to cope with the community and its people. The sad part is that, over time, you find out that your deceptive tactics partially work, and the more time that passes, the easier it is to use these tactics, until you get ridiculous with it. However, as always, you are the only one who can't see it; all you see is improvement on your polishing it up. What's worse is that the person you have to be at work eventually becomes "you" more than you're willing to admit. People notice this, and though you think that you can easily turn it off and on, keeping your workplace and your personal life separate, you can't. It's not that you literally can't transform, but that it becomes a characteristic of yours to be more aggressive in a negative way, because you get results that way.

You also have to remember that the adrenaline rush you receive while at work plays a major role in how you view work, and although the way you get the adrenaline may be negative, it may be needed! You get hooked on the adrenaline rush and block out how you obtained it. The negative domino effect continues, because now you've graduated to a sadder stage—respect out of fear.

When certain individuals seem to respect you, but you know it's because they fear you or are intimidated by you, you've lost the initial honor that made you join the force, and you yourself have taken this away. Illegal searches, roughing people up, making deals, pocketing money, and threatening people may all seem too far-fetched to the white-collar communities, but this is real and it's happening. The sad part is that the cops who do this (not to call them good cops) were decent people who get caught up in an ideology of how they're supposed to act at work, and get carried away! It's important for those cops who use these negative tactics to realize that being a cop is all about earning respect the right way. When the community that you vow to serve and protect fears your policing, your safety is questioned. More so, the small percentage of negative cops in America have truly damaged the reputations of positive, hardworking police officers who get results by doing an excellent job, as hard as it may be.

Here's the dilemma: nowadays, since race relations are strained, and you're taking a gang (because that's all the police force is, a registered organized gang) into the ghetto, supposedly to clean it up and stop the violence, you're taking mostly white, legal, hardworking cops and pitting them (in their minds) against minority, illegal, lower-class street people. It becomes too far-fetched (two different worlds), impossible for us to relate to one another without some type of force, some type of strategy, some type of extra scheme to beat the culprit at his game.

This is not the answer. In fact, each individual cop will have to come up with his own answer. But what I'm offering are suggestions and alternatives for both sides.

What I would like these police officers to realize is that you're going into a community and the crime may be high, but it's because the community is in search of money. The entire operation, from the drug dealer, to the pimp, to the stickup artist, to the drug user revolves around money. These people, before they were pimps, gang members, or drug dealers, were and still are people in search of money. They live in a poor, unstable community and are trying to survive in it. Though money may be the root of evil, it's not the money; it's how you get the money. The same for the cops; it's not that a community hates you for the job that you're doing, it's how you're doing it! Cops need to spend more time in the community they patrol, being a part of that community, but it will never happen. For two reasons:

1. Police stations (on down the line to government funding) won't want to shell out the extra money for cops to have block parties, meetings, dances, raffles, community marches, rallies, programs, or anything that will bring the cops closer to the community they patrol—too costly, and in fear of getting friendly with those they are supposed to be busting.

2. This falls on the cop, because the cop won't want to do this anyway (get involved with his patrolled area). He doesn't live in this area. Why put all this time into a community that's not his?

If you want to know the truth, they never put cops on beat in the community they live in (in the inner city), for fear of their personal life, home, and family. It shouldn't be like this. Can you imagine how valuable cops could be to their own neighborhoods if they were on beat there, were respected there, and went by the book? Neighborhoods would flourish, crime would lower, and America itself would be in a progressive stage. But there are some obstacles.

For one, since we know the ghettos are predominantly minority, to hire only that minority to work that area would be severely segregating areas of cities (once again).

Secondly, the areas that many white cops live in are low crime rate areas, and there's not a large demand for officers in these areas.

Thirdly, there are incidents of racial discrimination within the police force that haven't been fully handled yet, so immediate concerns need to be addressed first.

Lastly, the government funding being provided to the force is being mismanaged and directed toward more police cars, precincts, software, and firearms intended for policing an area, and not enough funds going to helping the area. So if you can't help the area, the crime rises, you continue searching for your adrenaline, and you marvel at the new Kevlar bulletproof vest the force handed out this morning! And the cycle continues.

New Era

New era police (mostly inner-city cops) have incorporated new tactics to get their brownie points in their **moving up the ladder** status. For instance, one major tactic is the **gun syndrome**. This is when a cop is about to falsely lock you up (already intimidating you, because he starts off threatening to place a sack of cocaine rocks that is not yours in your possession), but then offers you freedom in return for a gun! This is crazy! Because the cop is now the bad guy, holding the innocent person by the balls. Think about it. Here you are, walking down the street, and the cops roll up. They jump out, grab you, slap the handcuffs on you, and throw you in the back seat. They pull out a sandwich bag full of crack and demand that you manifest a gun (no matter if it's yours, a friend's, or from the house of anyone you know who has one) or you'll be taken in for drug selling. What! You see, this is why "the game" has been screwed up on both ends; the new era cops have dug deeper into BS with intimidating tactics, hence the new era young adults (whether innocent or not) have related to **tricking** to get out of trouble—meaning, even the intimidated young adult is in the wrong because the cops have forced him to tell on his friends, family, or whoever he knows has a gun. And he does. Morals out the window! You see, when my generation came up, street ethics were fair on both sides of the fence; it was a fair cat and mouse game. The police knew you sold drugs, and there was always an unspoken agreement that if they caught you with it, you were going down; if they didn't, then they'd try harder next time—because it was my job to stay one step ahead of them. If I allowed myself to get caught (with all the supposed security I had, and lookout tactics), then it was my realization that I had slipped and allowed them the upper hand. It was fair, with no extra worries of crooked police putting drugs on me and/or demanding guns. And there was definitely no snitching! (The old phrase "If you can't do the time, don't do the crime" meant something.)

It wasn't until the end of the '90s and beginning of the 2000s that the gun syndrome got out of hand. I was attacked three times by police with the gun syndrome—that's probably why I went to the penitentiary three times.

This gun syndrome may seem like a scene out of a movie, but it's truly happening throughout America. It is. In fact, it's gotten to the point where young adults (mostly minorities, but some whites too) are purchasing handguns simply for this reason alone! Yes. They call them **throwaways**. Young adults are purchasing guns basically as an insurance policy in case the dirty cops pull it! Simply guns to give to the police! Wow, how profitable for the police; a no-lose situation. Either these victims tell on someone, or take the weight that's not theirs. And no one is checking on the authenticity of the guns that these police bring back to the station! Meaning, how the hell did they actually acquire these guns?

So, the catch-22 is that guns are being purchased (which continues to keep guns on the streets) and there's no 100 percent guarantee that once you give the dirty cop the gun he'll let you go. The odds may be slightly in your favor; however, I've seen guys give the police a gun, only to have the cop give them both the crack case **and** the gun case!

Now we have a younger generation snitching on each other (as a norm) to avoid jail, guns are plentiful, young adults are literally scared (and hate) the police, while the police misuse their authority, and often renege anyway once they get the gun—and to top it all off, this cycle continues without anyone doing shit about it!

I don't promote guns (nor will I ever), but in all fairness, if a homeowner in the suburbs or a rural area is allowed to own a piece, then by all means an inner-city homeowner should have double the capability! To that I say: In literal reality, guns in the inner city **would be expected to be** more abundant, for the purpose of defending your property from the crackheads that do home invasions, gang members, rapists, and basically all the negative riffraff that the crazy city brings your way—poverty brings tension, thus crime. My point is that young adults living in the inner city will obviously have easier access to guns (because the need is greater, as well as getting the cops off their back), but because of it they are tragically caught in a loop and will continue snitching, purchasing guns, and going to jail—until something is done.

So let's recap. Cops are moving up the ranks as long as they're bringing in guns—supposedly ridding the streets of guns. However, the method of doing so is illegal, and is actually promoting guns. Teenagers and young adults are snitching on each other to avoid taking a fall for something that's not theirs, guns are being purchased, cops are hated, jails are filling, and tension is rising against the police force—and the crooked cops have created it all.

This new era is not a good one, and change is inevitable—so produce it.

Hint to My Guys

I have been illegal, and it's no way to live. If you're in a situation where running from the police becomes acceptable, then you're not getting what life has to offer you, simply a tick for a tack—meaning, you're "ticking" (doing whatever illegal activity you have to do to get money) so that you're "tacking" (spending your money on what you feel is necessary to live) is justified, when in actuality you're still doing wrong, and having to constantly look over your shoulder because of it. Slanging that shit, as we both know, is an easy way to get ends, and I know you've become good at it and you feel that you have no choice. But the game is played out and the stakes are too high! Think about it. If you are slanging that shit to pay rent, a car note, and buy the baby some Pampers, what happens when you get popped? You're sitting in jail, your rent still has to be paid, you don't have anyone you can depend on for the car note, and "somebody" has to step in and help your baby's mama with the Pampers! Hmm. So that's the risk you take. In fact, I'm not even saying don't sell drugs. My goal is for you to say it yourself!

***

Coming up in the ghetto, and having my children born in the ghetto, has interested me in how we both view cops.

As a parent, I try to be the humanitarian and instill what needs to be instilled. However, it sometimes goes against **what is** and what they see themselves. My children, along with other children, play in the community and watch as cops screech up, leap out of their cars, grab someone, search him, smack him, and let him go. This is the norm in the ghetto; it just is. Those the police intimidate and mess with are someone's big brother, someone's son, and possibly someone's father. So as kids watch, they can relate. As the cops leave, the kids hear the frustration and anger from the victim cursing the police. And they understand why he's mad, they didn't see him do anything wrong. Often kids see the police chase someone they know, beat him up if they catch him, handcuff him, and take him away.

So my children, along with others, grow up with this altered vision of what's supposed to be right, as opposed to what they see. I often talk with my children, explaining why the cops were chasing someone, trying to explain what he could have done wrong, but getting stuck when they ask, "Well, why did they beat him up, Daddy?" I can't make excuses for crooked cops, nor will I. So now the conversation turns to the cops; I try to justify and make it as understandable to my son as possible, feeling cheated because no matter what I said, I couldn't justify their actions.

The ghetto is real, and so are the cops and the people they chase. The cop going into the ghetto needs to understand that the people you chase are chasing something you're not—a dream. A dream that they can one day make it out of the ghetto. Doing what has not been fully thought out yet, that's why it's a dream. So by selling drugs or doing whatever it takes, the dream is still alive because it's the only thing they have to hold on to that seems real. And whether you like it or not, you are an obstacle blocking them from it. It's not that you're trying to be father fate, because what they are doing is wrong. We understand this. But don't go out of your way to be a negative factor in how you arrest them! Two wrongs don't make a right.

With the twenty-first century here, cops have to regain their moral and supportive structure in society. In fighting with this, they have to maneuver against an ever-changing society: Rock-and-Roll and Rap records against their tactics, badmouthing from the news and media, other crooked cops, community marches against them, and personal values that alter the way they work. If you're not cut out for the job of being part of the solution, do us a favor and leave the force because you've become part of the problem. Really.

So, the next time you roll up on that jive-ass pimp wannabe drug dealer, thinking he's so cool, remember one thing: he's just like you. He thinks you're unreal, bullshit, and too far-fetched. Try something new that I guarantee will flip his wig and gain the respect you deserve. Give him respect first, instead of hollering at him to come to the car or chasing him, simply talk to him. Because he's real, show him that you are real, too. Kick it with him, showing him that you understand where he's coming from. At first this technique might throw some people off, maybe shock them into being quiet (not the response you may be seeking because you want some immediate results), but keep it real with them, as you would like it, and I guarantee that by your third encounter with these individuals, they'll see you more as a real person instead of just a bothersome, ignorant cop. It pays to be you, because that is who you are, and the results are of willingness rather than force. Get the respect you deserve the right way.

Let us remember that in order for you to get ahead, in all actuality there is no "us" and "them." We are more "them" than we're giving credit to, and they are more "us" than we're willing to admit.

CABRINI GREEN

Where O Where is my neighborhood, Where O Where can it be?
Is that you? Cabrini, come on out girl, show the world who you really
are…a buck wild superstar!

This is the opening and chorus stanza of one of my poems about Cabrini (I literally have hundreds of them). It describes perfectly my search for and realization of my community. The reason I'm adding this chapter to the book is because Cabrini Green in America is the mother of all housing projects (so they say). The reform implementation (including demolition), if successful here, will be carried out nationwide; Cabrini being the initial example. The problem is that though they're trying to say Cabrini is the prime target, they've already started revitalizing in four major cities, not to mention the other housing projects here in Chicago.

For years, the city and **the powers that be** have been trying to get rid of Cabrini. Cabrini sits on some prime land as far as Chicago's geographical makeup: Two blocks in either direction are three major train lines; three major bus lines run through Cabrini; it's three blocks from the Gold Coast; three from the downtown area; three from Lincoln Park; four from the Lincoln Park Zoo; and four from the Lakefront! Cabrini is based in the middle of Chicago, thus offering the mobile benefits other communities don't have.

Cabrini is a city within a city. It's sad to say, but there are many people who have stayed in Cabrini for years without leaving the community. There are five churches, four regular stores, one supermarket (including a meat market), four elementary schools (one being Catholic), three day care centers and preschools, three barber shops (two of them being home shops), two clinics, one WIC place, a dollar store, two restaurants (including pager and cell phone companies inside the restaurants—of course!), three parks, two baseball fields, four community centers, one recording studio, one cab stand, two fire stations, one brand-new police station, and people selling whatever you need from the streets to their homes—it's available.

So it's evident why the powers that be want this area. It offers white-collar society an advantage to their assets: downtown, the Gold Coast, Lakefront, the zoo, and everything else within the community. Before I get a little deeper into the reform implementation of Cabrini, I'd just like to say that Cabrini's reform (though America would like you to think it represents all housing projects) is simply that—a reform. It's not a reform for the housing projects; it's a reform for what each city feels it can benefit from the reform itself. So Cabrini, along with other housing projects, is in for a disastrous change. I can't speak for each individual housing project. Maybe some do need change, due to actual living conditions, crime, or circumstance, but with reform, it's how you reform that makes all the difference in the world! You have to include the people, the ones who've been living there for years—the ones who make up the community—the people, the people, the people! And in Cabrini, the people speak out because they've been misjudged and mistreated for so long. When you have a community that at least comes together in times of crisis, that's a good sign. This is a key component for housing projects to administer, because strength in numbers is what's needed when demolition or reform is at hand! If the money has already been provided and you're waiting to see who's going to do the reform, I say this to other housing projects: Don't let the city pick the architectural firms (or contractors). If they're moving you out, they at least owe you the respect of input into who gets picked. They owe you that much.

(Will the Real Architects Please Stand Up?)

Major cities want their inner area back, moving housing developments and their people to the suburbs. There are two reasons this hasn't happened yet:

1. The cities simply don't have the finances yet to carry it through.
2. People in the suburbs are scared stiff of this progression, and are the ones working in the city, so they're not going to be too quick to have anyone move by them yet.

Before and during the demolition in Cabrini, there were literally hundreds of architectural firms that wanted to be hired for the redevelopment plan. Every one submitted, and though the city looked over all of them, it was evident that they were going to pick a certain company. However, there was one company that should have been picked, not just by the city but because they had the backing of the community—Landon Architects.

Landon is not a large company, as was the one that was chosen, nor is it as impersonal, and that's what made all the difference in the world.

Landon Architects, owned by Peter Landon, sits at 314 West Institute Place, which is practically across the street from Cabrini. I received a call from Peter during the demolition; he not only wanted to meet with me and the staff of the *Voices* newspaper, but he wanted to hold weekly meetings in Cabrini to show his plan to residents. Also, he wanted to run ads in the newspaper to talk about the weekly meetings and to discuss Landon's ideas for the community. I'll admit that at first, being the editor of *Voices* and a community figure, I thought he was just another outsider trying to fit in, especially with the architectural competition in full swing. So I did my homework.

Peter has a close-knit staff of good people; people who are warm, who enjoy their jobs, who came into the community without him, and continued to do so even after their company wasn't chosen. I wrote an editorial in January's issue of *Voices*, talking about the redevelopment plan. In one paragraph, I stated, "In reference to those interested, we will be placing different architectural firms' ideas and layouts in upcoming issues of *Voices* to give you an idea of their plans (if their firm gets picked to do the remodeling). This is our way of keeping you apprised on what's going on and to see each one of these different avenues and ideas." Sadly and surprisingly, though we received several calls from different architectural firms, Landon was the only one that placed an ad. Landon was the only one that came into the community, Landon was the only one that gave us a grant before and after the firms were chosen, Landon was the only one that opened their phone lines to the community, and Landon still has ties to the community.

Landon Architects had a community-based solution that had a cooperative workshop plan, a home ownership opportunity plan, and a site and home design plan. For weeks on end, they came to us with pictures, drawings, blueprints, plans, and ideas, and listened to community involvement, and responded.

"The current Cabrini situation is bad for the city of Chicago. Cabrini Green is a community; and, as with any community that has been intact for a period of time, it has created a social structure that provides stability, leadership and agencies for help. The city of Chicago, as a whole must support its many neighborhoods, bringing them together and allowing the intricate mingling of diversity to flourish. This diversity, particular identities and the agencies of the communities of Chicago is what makes our city beautiful.

"When market rate development moves into a lower area, there is almost no chance for the existing rental structure to maintain affordability over the long run. The new Housing and Associated commercial development of the Hope VI program will inevitably raise taxes and, in turn, raise the rent structure, ultimately displacing many of the older residents. The only way for the existing population to maintain a presence in an escalating neighborhood is for the existing community to be able to establish an equity position in both the existing and new real estate. For this to happen, there must be options for equity interest in both the older and new buildings. There must be affordable ownership and rental opportunities, as well as a community support network available to direct the residents to those options.

"We believe that with positive and committed leadership within the community, support from the city and its agencies, creative development and financial planning, and sound architectural design and land planning, a housing program that will satisfy the Hope VI RFP, provide affordable home ownership options and community redevelopment programs for the residents of Cabrini can be provided.

"Our objective is to step-up the quality of life for those families being relocated from high-rise public housing and to integrate these families into an economically diverse community."

This was their opening statement to us, not only as a community but as a person who made up the community; there's a difference. Landon also wanted us to remember that people are people; you cannot be impersonal when dealing with a community, especially coming from the outside and having to gain trust during the start of a relationship. Thus the relationship grew. Everybody wanted the grant from Hope VI, but nobody went about it the right way except Landon Architects. I'm sincerely disappointed that the hardworking, good people at Landon weren't chosen. It would have been nice. We could have watched their small firm grow with us, our meetings could have grown bigger, and the jobs they talked about could have changed some lives. Our relationship would have been a long one, and though they still have ties with us, there's nothing for them to really do in Cabrini Green, and we understand that. We wish them the best of luck in becoming the immense architectural firm they deserve to be. Don't change, Landon, you're a good company.

(CABRINI, Where are you?)

When I came from the penitentiary in August of '95, I came home to the *Voices of Cabrini* newspaper. I resurrected the paper with the help of Peter Benkendorf, an outsider who had the interest of the community at heart, and who invisibly became my knight in shining armor. He had previously started the paper with Mark Pratt and Henrietta Thompson, its founders. Upon getting home, news of the *Voices* resurrection spread fast. Ben Jerovsky from the *Reader* newspaper came to follow me for two days, to write his column "Neighborhood News."

Voices was my life, and as I brought it back to life I beamed with triumph! It was literally all I had, coming home and wanting to do something positive for the hood. However, there were too many obstacles to face once it was underway.

Though the peace treaty between the gangs was supposedly intact, there was still shooting every night. This limited our stories, because although I was still ducking and dodging bullets to get a story, others wouldn't. My staff couldn't get paid (because we were a nonprofit), and though they said it didn't matter, I knew it was only a matter of time. Certain cops in the area didn't like the fact of a community newspaper because it exposed their dirt, so I started being harassed by these cops. "What do we gotta do, kick your ass to get in the newspaper?" they'd ask mockingly, pulling up to me. So-called "activists" in the neighborhood criticized the paper's plight because I had two outsiders helping push, yet these activists always wanted to be in the paper. We survived off strictly advertising, so staying afloat from month to month was a struggle. I had to distribute the papers myself, which is hard as hell in a trap-ass car, sometimes on foot. Everyone criticized what should be in the paper, yet few participated. We had a booth at Generation Expo, got a city web page, and an over flowing P.O. box, with no finances to follow up or pursue. Other organizations said they wanted to help financially, in return for controlling the paper. Outsiders couldn't believe Cabrini **had** a paper at all, it was too far-fetched. Was it a political forum? Was it a Hip-hop paper, was it militant, evangelic, or a cry for help? What was *Voices?* In the end, I was doing the Jamaican thing, literally too much work. I took the pictures, wrote the stories, held the meetings, edited the material, made the calls, did the layout, interviewed, distributed, solicited, faxed, e-mailed, begged, and most of all, "followed up" over and over again! (If it wasn't for the help of Peter Benkendorf, and certain individuals of his Magnani team, I would have folded much sooner). Bear in mind that this was new to me. But it was made for me, so I hung in there until I had no social life, no drive for work, no schedule, no routine, no nothing but *Voices.*

I sat in my Cabrini apartment, staring at my computer. Harry Porterfield from Channel 7 had just left after taping his "Someone You Should Know" segment. Though I was delighted to be the subject and do the piece, I didn't feel worthy; I was physically burnt out. Every day I wanted to walk away from the paper, and every day I came close. I could barely keep up with anything. I would go to bed thinking about how I could get money for the paper, I'd wake up with it on my mind. A friend would try to get it off my mind by taking me out clubbing, but everything was about the paper. I'd get to the club and all I could think about was getting the manager of the club to run an ad, maybe two ads; hell, I'd give him a discount in exchange for coupons in the paper to his club! I went to the Harold Washington Library to start grants, all the colleges, the black pages, radio stations, Hip-hop events, seminars, churches, millionaires, organizations, strangers, studios, lawyers, the Internet, even funeral homes. And my P.O. box was full of mail from Texas to Canada, from other housing developments wanting advice and help on starting their own community newspaper.

So as I sat in my apartment, staring at the computer, my eyes focused on the monitor and the VOC letters that covered the screen as wallpaper. The screen seemed to stare back at me, and the letters VOC (and what they meant) echoed in my mind—*Voices of Cabrini, Voices of Cabrini, Voices*—and I stood up. If *Voices of Cabrini* stood for anything, it was just that; the community had one last chance to help me with this paper, because it was "OUR" paper and I needed them. Thus, my attention returned to the neighborhood and the resources we had.

The problem with Cabrini is that everybody claims to be broke, times are rough, and everyone has it worse than the next man! People are quick to say who else has money and criticize them if they don't give it up! Cabrini agencies want you to promote their services, yet they won't drop a penny! Cabrini's so-called "activists" claim to be broke, yet they drive around in Cadillacs! Cabrini's store owners (mostly Arab) claim to be broke, but buy hot merchandise from the dope fiends all day long! The major drug dealers promised the world, but when it was time to collect they ducked and dodged! Once, I asked one of the prettiest girls in the land to dress sexy and get an ad from the Arab who owned the supermarket—it worked. He bought a whole page, but when he found out that he couldn't get a date with her (she was sixteen and he was forty-nine), he wouldn't even talk with us for months. He had played **himself**. So this is what I faced in the neighborhood, and though I struggled, it was evident; I was losing my identity trying to hold on to the paper. I wanted Cabrini to be one person, I wanted to be able to talk to this person and make her realize the tool we had, but I couldn't. The community had failed me. In January of '98, the paper folded, two and a half years after I got out.

Looking back, I saw what an asset the paper had been, not just to the community but to me. After going through a guilt trip for a couple of months—because you have to realize, I had ended up representing the paper, and the paper represented a young adult whom I had cared for from birth, taking the time and patience in molding him, step by step, paying attention and raising him, he actually had a life; he did—I let the community know that the paper had died. All of a sudden, everybody and their mama wanted to help, but it was too late, I had washed my hands. Besides, I knew Cabrini all too well; these were simply desperate cries of nothing; to hold on to an invisible dream, their own guilty consciences were speaking out. It was over, and I was free.

The community (and the cops) looked at me as being an activist or a community leader, but this was not my intention. Not that many people knew I had just come home from the joint, I was just a street kid trying to do something positive with my life. The paper put me hands-on with the shit I needed to stay positive! With the paper I counted in society, and went from ex-con to public official. I met people in the mayor's office and rubbed elbows with city and state officials. Carol Mausley Braun sent letters to me, along with every alderman and representative of Chicago. Ed Walsh from the *Washington Post* called me (even came to the hood), as well as Juanitta White from the *Chicago Tribune*. Kevon Smith at Island Recorders was inspired by my commitment to the hood and offered me free studio time to lay some tracks. Ronnit Desilou, a student at Columbia College, wanted to do a documentary on Cabrini and asked for my help; her video is now done and has been on PBS (it, too, is entitled *Voices of Cabrini*). I taught myself how to type, learned computers, and became friends with the folks at News web (where *Voices*, along with the *Reader*, was printed). Gang leaders from around the city put down their guns, animosities, and slanging to give me support as we networked on marches, rallies, and community activism. The radio stations gave me private line numbers to get through and I talked on-air. The paper was used as a vehicle to meet and interview celebrities. And most of all. *Voices* helped me meet people who became good friends from their involvement in the paper: Godfrey Bey, whose "Come and Get It" food section helped him in other avenues of work; Shanita Bishop's "A Person Perspective" was from a strong sista's point of view and in demand by many; Mark Pratt, who help start the paper, returned with deep columns and became a substitute teacher; Michel "Hassan" Smith and Kino, two strong incarcerated men who sent us articles from the penitentiary; Jimmy Williams, who owned "Abstracts" T-Shirt Company; Malik Yusef, who made sure he never missed a deadline with some slammin' poetry; Lorenzo Hickey, AKA "Rockin' Renzo," kept us in tune with the R & B and Hip-hop scene; Peter Benkendorf, the man behind the scenes, who kept in touch with me from the penitentiary and allowed me the dream of launching my paper; Troy Parham, a good friend who was there just about the entire time (we even ended up dubbing him business manager) and taught me the meaning of patience; Ken Smith, who took the time to teach me how to lay out; Cynthia Parker, The Deacon, Joe Perry, Walter Burnette Jr., Tyrone Randolph. and all those kids (especially the kids) who contributed stories, poems, ideas, art, and inspiration!

It's easy for many to say that outsiders aren't a part of Cabrini, but the sad reality is that they are. These are the ones who get involved when many of us won't. And in a way, we can't say it's sad because this is what we need in America, communities and people reaching out to others communities that need it. I think with Cabrini it was a pride thing, and nobody wants to admit they need help—this is the attitude I had to deal with.

When *Voices* first started, one of the main things we didn't have was office space; everything was done from my apartment. And though people promised us office space, rec sites, and community centers, it was all talk. If I were now to resurrect *Voices*, it would work. I know what needs to be done, the finances would be available, and the community would support it. I would love to see *Voices* flourish, not just in Cabrini (what's left of it) but citywide. However, the truth of the matter is, I simply haven't the time. *Voices* has to be nurtured, motivated, upheld, respected, pampered, cultivated, and glorified! It's a seed waiting to sprout, and could go in a remarkable direction. If any young person is physically and mentally ready (with a small team, equally determined), I dare you to give me a call. I will be just as excited to start as you are.

I often sat at my desk asking myself, "Cabrini, where are you?" Eventually I knew the answer; she was with me all along, she just didn't know how to speak out! There were many who never heard of *Voices*, and how could they? It was a small paper. But it represented a good side of what people wanted. Though the community physically wasn't capable of strong support, they mentally craved the paper. It represented a hurting community and is a part of Cabrini history that spoke for all of us.

(I Love Cabrini, but hate it!)

I love Cabrini because we're a community that thrives on each other, but I hate it because we do just as much gossiping about each other. I love Cabrini because there's something happening twenty-four hours a day, but I hate it because many children are there to witness it. I love Cabrini because we have the best parties in the world, but I hate it because there's often someone starting some shit. I love Cabrini because we have some of the smartest, hardcore men and women on the face of this earth, but I hate it because they end up either in jail or dead, not knowing how to focus. I love Cabrini because you can get rich off a dice game, but I hate it because you make enemies. I love Cabrini because it has some of the baddest cars in Chicago, but I hate it because they never cruise off the land. I love Cabrini because I can go into any building and find a candy house, but I hate it because it's usually on a high floor and the elevators don't work. I love Cabrini because of our location in Chicago, but I hate it because a lot of residents don't take advantage of it. I love Cabrini because my kids live there with me, but I hate it because my kids live there with me…

(OUR LANDMARK)

Cabrini Green, as we all know, is famous, but for what? Well, the news and media give us the impression that it's notoriously violent; others will say it's poverty, some will say it's location, a few will say it's deaths, and most will say it's gangs and drugs. WOW! No wonder former mayor Jane Byrne temporarily moved in; she was going to change all that, right? Wrong.

Cabrini Green has three parts that were built over a twenty-year span: First, in 1942 came the "Frances Homes," which are two-flat walk-ups including a basement apartment, which we call the **Rowhouses**. Then there were the "Cabrini Extensions" built in 1958, which had two parts, North and South (the north we call the **Boulevard** and the south we call the **Wild End**; however, they were both called **The Reds** because of the actual red brick color; it's just that you had to be specific as to what part in The Reds you were going to. Then finally, in 1962 came the "William Green Homes," better known to us as **The Whites** because of the beige/off-white brick color. Eventually, the entire area was known as Cabrini Green. Cabrini's large area is round, giving it more of a community effect rather than in a straight row, as other housing projects are situated. When Cabrini was first built, the area was mostly Italian, with few blacks. Secretary of State Jesse White (who the Italians nicknamed **Bucky**) grew up in this area, and to this day still keeps in touch with many of his Italian friends. By the '60s, many of the Italians had moved westward and Cabrini became predominantly black. Cooley High School was famous for its wild and rebellious teens, and was the target of Michael Schultz, who directed *Cooley High*. Many of the residents were cast as stand-ins, even major parts, but barely got paid. There was supposed to be a sequel to *Cooley High*, people even signed their names to be in it, but it never happened. Curtis Mayfield came out of Cabrini Green and went to the top of the charts in 1972 with his *Superfly* soundtrack album. A skinny Jimmy Walker, who played J.J Evans on *Good Times*, stands in his Cabrini Green apartment and faces Janet Jackson, hollering "Dynomite!" Then came *Heaven's a Playground, Whiteboyz, Hoop Dreams* and *Candy Man*, all of which were filmed in Cabrini. Hall of famer Herb Kent (infamous DJ and pioneer of the term "Dusty's") from V103 used to DJ in Cabrini's Lower North Center back in the '60s. R. Kelly and Nas shot their "Street Dreamers" video in Cabrini, as well as Cash Money which shot some of their video there too. Author Bruce Conn (who still lives in Cabrini) wrote *Horrors of Cabrini*. Sugar Ray Dinky (who came out with **Cabrini Green Rap** and numerous commercials) was one of Chicago's pioneers of rap, hailing from Cabrini. Episodes of *The Awakening* have been filmed in Cabrini, along with celebrities stopping in the Cabrini to promote new Movies and CDs, and to sign autographs. The infamous Peace Treaty in '92 started in Cabrini and spread citywide, when Dantrell Davis got shot on October 13th while going to school. Even when the Peace Treaty broke everywhere else throughout the city, it remained solid in Cabrini for six years! The Jesse White Tumblers hail from Cabrini. Cabrini parties are the best underground parties I've been to, anywhere. On summer nights, you can walk through Cabrini with friends and simply enjoy the community. Everyone knows you, people are having fun, and you're at home. By the time you read this, the new police station will have been completed, on the corner of Larrabee and Division. The community as we once knew it will change, the presence alone of this high-tech station will cause tension, bringing in police officers under false pretenses. It's too bad. Cabrini is such a rich and vibrant community with such a mysterious overtone. Those outside, who have been in the community, can relate. The next time you're driving by Cabrini in your little Audi, don't be relieved that the police station is there; be disappointed, because it's a statement that says so much.

I'll leave you with this poem I wrote for a place I will always cherish. Good or bad, it's what made my community special. Though you may see the artifacts still standing as you pass by, it will never be the same. Goodbye, Cabrini Green, you will be missed dearly by those who were there.

Shadows create shadows, and lost shadows create nothingness,

I remember when the shadows were full. I remember. I remember when castles were sturdy and prominent, so dominant, so real.

When structure lit the hallways and ramps with sun rays, creating good days.

When walks through the hood were good walks, with daps and talks, though po-po's hawked and girlfriends stalked, we parked and wanged in the lot.

Old faces coming home from doing new numbers; happy to be on the bricks, in yet new bricks and yet old bricks...

Little shining stars stay out under the twinkling stars, until the twinkling stars blend and disappear, and the little stars branded with yet more scars, slowly lost their shine.

When building counts were full and Sunday was unity day,

Fifteen cars deep we were off the land energized like foreplay.

Mondays were like Saturdays, and Saturdays were better than Mondays!

Thunder clapped like clockwork, when there was no rain,

And blue light parties created new seeds more shopping for new last names

Beef was rare, but when present, was handled like true warriors

Rare did we leave the land, but when we did, explored like Tom Sawyer!

My neighborhood was a landmark, famous throughout nations

My neighborhood was a sad part of my endeavor's creation.

Where O Where
Is My Neighborhood

****

AFTERMATH

While writing this book, much demolition has taken place in Cabrini; it is almost gone. Out of a once thriving, twenty-seven high-rise building community (including row houses), only six remain with occupants—three of those will be slated for demolition at the end of this month, and more are slated in the coming months. Cabrini is now a ghost town.

RESPECT

Who would have thought thirty years ago that someone was going to write a chapter in a book about respect, especially within races. Maybe on how races should respect each other, during the civil rights movement , or even the issue of respect of self (and, to a certain extent, some of this chapter will be dealing with that), but I'd like to discuss respect in its individual racial authenticity and how it's viewed, given, related, and perceived.

When mainstream whites grow up, they grow up in a world where respect, means just that. You've channeled your respect on a gradual process through the years: Your teachers in school undoubtedly got much of your respect, your parents received the utmost respect, your coworkers and employers were given respect at the various jobs you held, police officers were given a great deal of respect. Neighbors, senior citizens, friends, parents of friends, PTA, pastor, doctor, grocer, dentist, drill sergeant, and down the line, of all the extra people you had to encounter during your busy weeks, that turned into months, that turned into years. Their lives have stability in advancement. Thus, respect is also learned as an aging tool. You learn over the years how to use it, channel it, accept it, dismiss it, create it, and strengthen it. Respect becomes an implanted device in subconscious thinking.

When blacks grow up, it's usually in single-parent homes, plus families are larger, so respect is divided. As you get older in the hood, respect is based on two things:
1. Money (people's finances)
2. Fear (people's reputations)

People's money (and status quo) gains respect through your perception of how they hold on to it. Because managing money when you don't have that much is a hard task, you tend to splurge on the things you want because you know the money is going to be gone soon. Too, the things you show with the money you have create respect—a nice car, jewelry, clothes, and many of the material things we feel get us noticed in society. That's why drug dealers get respect in the hood, because they've learned how to manage money and often do little things for the neighborhood. They also get respect because many drug dealers are feared.

Fear in the community comes from drug dealers, gang members, and basically brothers who have a reputation for being on some buck-wild shit. Nine times out of ten, drug dealers are gang members, so their reputations have to be "known" in order to be successful or it leaves room for the next man to get on top of him. Having a known reputation means you've shot someone, physically harmed someone, kidnapped, stabbed, etc.—and all the hood knows about it. In doing so, you create a reputation that others fear. Thus, you've earned respect.

So, blacks in the ghetto have a different image of respect, simply because it's a different environment. If you're not going to school anymore, you don't have to deal with teachers. If your parents are on drugs, why respect them? If you're not working, who gives a damn? If the police chase you and kick your ass, screw them, too. Your neighbors have no respect for you, so why should you have any for them? You have little contact with senior citizens so they're out of the picture. Your friends are in gangs; their parents are some of your best customers. PTA who? You don't go to church; you got kicked off your mama's HMO card; grocer? You wouldn't even know where to look for a dentist; drill sergeant who?

Your little world in actuality revolves around self, because you literally don't have contact with the basics that whites have. Respect can't have the same meaning. And this is also how your love gets diluted with respect. If many of your contacts are your gang affiliation friends, then any thing or gesture done by them out of kindness is gratefully received, because emotional responses in your life are limited. Thus, you acknowledge the slightest gestures (a little money, or a sack of crack to sell) are absorbed as love. Remember, you also fear this person, so it's easy for him to open the door to your acceptance. It's like the famous case of the battered wife; she loves him out of fear, and any little gesture he offers is accepted wholeheartedly and perceived as love. She's isolated and feels there's nothing else available to her. This is basically the same environment response.

(Holding On)

Now I will get more detailed. With the actual black street male, when dealing with respect there is a syndrome called "holding on." But **holding on** is more of a self issue, concerning the perception of how you deal with others perceiving you, which in turn reflects upon self and how you accept and deal with self. Understand? It's like this: say, for instance, that you are a brotha from the ghetto, and while coming up you were buck wild, creating a name for yourself. Everyone respected you, whether from fear or because of the many things you accomplished. Then you moved out of town—it doesn't matter why (running from the police, from gang bangers, for a job, etc.)—and moved back to the hood one year later. Upon returning, you will be treated differently—meaning, your respect level has diminished. You literally will have to check out your surroundings, see what's happening, and start all over again. It's just that simple. The hood waits for no one.

The problem with this is that urban minorities are taught from the time they are young to be buck wild to gain respect; therefore, moving out of the ghetto is a break from **being ghetto**—and is invisibly looked upon as being soft, that you obviously couldn't make it in the hood. Brothas will die to show others that they're still down—especially for the hood. And this literally tears apart the self-perception of what you've been taught since you were little—meaning, to have moved out of the hood and gotten another taste of a more positive reality—embedding morals—attaches foreign newness. You're a fish out of water. Though you want to be productive in society, it is still not your complete reality, and you somehow know that it will never be. Whites don't realize that in the hood, peer pressure is not looked upon at all like it is in the white arena. Remember, in the white arena, peer pressure is looked upon as doing something you know that you have no business doing, but doing it because you feel pressured to by your peers. In the ghetto arena, the amount of time is all that is recognized; meaning, the issue is not whether you'll do it or not, but how soon: sell drugs, smoke, gangbang, have kids, get a rep, etc. This attached concept pursues you through life.

You had better hold on to those buck-wild bursts of energy that whisper that you are a power to be reckoned with. It's interesting, because a large component and source of the **holding on** concept derives from adrenaline. **Holding on** is a constant battle with self, it is the acceptance of self to the whole—you to your environment. To lose your respect and reputation is to lose yourself. You literally become your own peer pressure. This is why many white people view most street brothas as these hardcore, not-giving-a-damn entities. There is something going on that whites need to understand about the ghetto persona, and it is called **holding on**.

(Ratt vs. Cannon)

Times have changed, even in the ghetto. Two great men who once reigned over Cabrini Green in the '80s and '90s are chilling out now. Long live Ratt and Cannon, two good friends of mine. During their time of reign (these men had great power on the street level), they were respected by all on the land. But as things died out for them, so did the fear, and in turn the respect.

The thing that made both men unique was their age. They were in their forties, and were not looked upon as the younger men of today. Each had his way of running things and each was going to make sure the job got done. Though the men reigned at different times, they disliked each other, each having different ideas of how shit should be run. But there was always mutual respect between them.

"As the young men of today take over, they have to realize that getting respect out of fear will never last like getting respect by your accomplishments," said Cannon, as we were on our way to the player's ball. He continued, "The problem is that what kind of accomplishments can you really do when you've never really been anywhere or have any type of creativity?" This is true. And if we (those in the hood) continue to let others fall into this false pretense of respect, and what it's supposed to be, then we've bullshitted ourselves, the community, and those who believe it. What the hell is the good in having an insight into something if we don't let others know about it?

Ratt, a few friends, and I went backstage to go see rapper Too Short. Before we got in, we noticed a fight breaking out near the back entrance. "See, that's the problem with the younger brothers out here now," stated

Ratt. "Brothers don't understand that respect is needed to make order. Without order, there's no structure; we ain't got shit."

Though Ratt and Cannon didn't see eye to eye and didn't really fuck with each other, I was good friends with both of them and know how alike they really were. I could never have told them that at the time, because it's something they just wouldn't want to hear, but somehow I know that they knew it too. This goes to show the difference a couple of decades have made in the ghetto, especially with crack hitting the set.

Ratt and Cannon were pioneers of a certain "ghetto black culture" that they've withstood (they're not dead or in jail for life) and survived. They've paid their dues and now simply want to relax. My question is this: If you've put in all this work for your thang and you're still alive, shouldn't that alone be enough for brothers to respect you?

***

While I was writing this book, Cannon has recently become President of the LAC (Local Advisory Council) in Cabrini. This is a major step in showing the community and youth (what's left of it) the importance of political power. Cannon has not only stood the test of time, but switched a negative into a positive, while still earning respect—something quite rare in the ghetto.

***

(TOES and TERMS)

Stepping on toes was a big issue in the late '80s and early '90s. There were no questions asked when someone accidentally stepped on your new sneakers. You had just better be ready to fight! And it's important that people understand that in the ghetto another false identity was labeled as respect, and that was "disrespect."

When this happened, it immediately and falsely justified blatant actions. "Man, I stole on that Mark because he disrespected me and stepped on my shoes" or "I shot that vic because he disrespected us by wearing all that red on our set!" Somehow, disrespect has taken the place of respect, and respect is simply looked upon as your manhood. In the ghetto, your manhood is attacked if you've been disrespected, and this is perceived as a physical threat. Thus, the true concept of respect has been tampered with, so much so that there are all these different avenues.

Street terms such as "wiggers" and "white boys" are terms many of us have used before (some of us still might), but we've got to analyze these. There's a difference between a curse word and a stereotypical hate word. It may be hard for a white person to respect another white person who calls them a wigger when all that has been done is to replace an "n" with a "w." White society feels it's okay to say wigger because it's not the word nigger, and you're referring to whites. Well, what you're implying is that these whites act like niggers, but since they're white you'll call them wiggers. You're disrespecting them because they're not acting how whites are supposed to act (how you feel they're supposed to act). On the reverse side of this, whites who are in this so-called black world and have been labeled wiggers need to analyze their usage of the word "nigger." Being around blacks who may not mind you saying it can be a catch-22, because there will be times when others are around who may not feel comfortable with you, and your respect may get diminished. Don't get me wrong, it's cool that you're down like that, and I know you don't mean any harm, but we're in a transitional stage (here in America) where often it's not so much what you're saying, but who you're saying it around. Blacks, who are cool with whites who do this, need to pull them to the side, and inform them of this. It's not that big of an issue unless you make it so. Just be firm about it, and if they're really your guys, they'll understand. Now, it doesn't stop there. In order for the respect pattern to go all the way through, my brothers, my down-ass black brothers (and sistas) from the hood need to chill out on calling any male who is white a "white boy." This goes all the way back to the slave days, when white slave owners referred to Negro men as boys. Now that blacks have come all the way to the term "African Americans," it's as if blacks are, out of resentment, trying to belittle white men. If brothers don't like being referred to as "boys," it's simple: don't call anyone else one. (I realize that you don't mean any harm by it, but that's exactly how white's feel about certain terms they use toward you; that you feel offensive). When you respect others, it shows that you have the utmost respect for yourself.

(The N Word)

Much controversy has surrounded the "N" word here in America. We've dealt with it via books, talk shows, radio programs, comedy,

seminars, even the street corners, whe[...]
wrong individual, enticing controversy. I [...]
word "nigger," leaving you (regardless of you[...]
new ideology.

The word "nigger" in its present perception[...]
early slave trade, following it down through the south[...]
of course hatched and attached its negative connotati[...]
this word's residue continues to surface is because it has b[...]
immoral to continue using it, and yet it's flourishing in ou[...]
Therefore, regardless of morality, a force drives this particular word[...]
has it become bigger than Spic, Wop, Dago, and Chink? How has it b[...]
caught in our music, theater, television, and speech?

The first thing that is important for the reader to remember is the
bridge between street idealism and mainstream society. Regardless of
finances, a powerful urban perception that began in the sixties, and has
been following and growing throughout the years with aspects of Hip
Hop, has molded a new breed of black men (and women) who, although
they live within society, have their own styles of speech, clothing, music,
dance, and perception toward the whole. The "bridge" signifies the fact
that the two (certain blacks and whites) do indeed live within the same
society, but literally perceive their plight and contribution different and
apart. This new man, even when holding a prominent nine to five job,
does realize that he's a taxpayer, but feels unattached to mainstream
society because he feels those involved are not his caliber. Now, imagine
the black entity under this financial bracket—all the way to the ghetto,
those on welfare who truly feel inactive toward society. This large margin
of African American blood lives a literal life; meaning that sarcasm and
other pleasantries have no use in the mindset, nor are they wanted. How
can you have time to battle wits with frivolous sarcasm when your life
deals with literally making it from day to day? So the mind frame is
not geared to what society can tell them to do or say, because general
society appears fictitious. Growing up using the word nigger over and
over—even coming from the parents—is normal. And though some may
say that generations were ignorant or hoodwinked to have even started to
use this word many moons ago, and to continue to use it, that is not only
irrelevant (because what has been done, has been done), but is not looked
upon as such by blacks now. Blacks are aware of where it started, and that

re it was said by the supposedly
ill cover all the avenues of the
skin tone) with your own

has its roots in the
n colonies, which
n. The reason
en believed
society!
How
en

used on where the present
ned, they have taken over
ation. Period.
ed out here in America,
al word "nigger" that is
ow it started. Obviously,
by whites), there would
re is a word that went
e first actual intent was
Then came the second
ctual female, which has
using the word about
ay, I'm in bitch mode,
he television networks

and it became acceptable to use the B word. The N word started as a negative remark toward blacks, and the B word climbed from a female dog to a negative remark directed at the entire female race. This is not to say that the word bitch is equal in perception to nigger, because however you perceive this topic is personal, this only implies that the two words have made a climb from one aspect to another. The word nigger has not finished its climb (or descent, depending on how you view it), but it has started its journey in notification. This chapter is unbiased about society's decisions in this matter. The uncovering, and the goal of this segment, is to bring forth all that has to be done in moving ahead, not standing still, which is what we are doing with the N word in general society when we run in circles through the years, only focusing on its early negative connotation. In the previous segment, I briefly touched on the timing here in America, with whites saying the N word around and to their black friends, and the company that may or may not accept it. In which case, the black friends have to set the pace and decide if that location is appropriate or not. However, this word and concept, because the word has become its own concept, is accelerating so fast, that its acceptance is baffling. And of the other words (chink, wigger, white boy, spic, etc.), it is the only word that has achieved its peculiarity and continued to move ahead. Remember, this word (as any once demeaning word) is only as effective as we make it. More so, it is the only "once demeaning word" that the victims themselves now commonly use! You don't hear Latinos embracing the word spic and commonly calling each other that. But blacks have done this. What's even more baffling is that not only does the younger generation say it about themselves, they use it with everyone—all nationalities! This has broken new ground.

Now let's focus on the concept of moving from one aspect to another, because this is what's happening with the N word, although general society still seems to be chasing its tail. Those on the other side of the bridge not only embrace the N word among themselves, but also now have called their white friends the N word. I will use "nigga" through the rest of this segment, because the spelling is accurate for the pronunciation being used. Being called "nigga" in the streets is now as common as being called "brotha" or "homie." This is where the N word is moving from one aspect to another; meaning, mind frame and perception allow those who feel they own the word to make the rules! This is interesting in itself, because it allows the former underdog to control new ground, subliminally turning a negative into a positive. When you can call someone who is not black "nigga" because they are your friend, then you have amazingly squashed and denounced its formerly hated aspect. This is the present transition that this side of the bridge is witnessing, which leaves general society to ponder the question: "How can something so perplexing be combated with such a twist of fate, and so simple?"

There's another unique aspect that surrounds this once hated word! I recently came home from the penitentiary, where I was locked up with professional blacks and whites ranging from bankers and brokers to lawyers and accountants, as well as big-time drug lords to drug addicts, each using the N word at random—everyone, and never in a negative way. In fact, there is something else interesting that I noticed while incarcerated.

Since we can't change the world overnight, there will obviously be instances where the N word is said in a demeaning way. This happened in the penitentiary twice, and once in a lounge. The first incident was white officers hollering at black inmates in a way that Martin Luther King Jr. himself would not have turned the other cheek. And yet these inmates, who were huge and could have pummeled the officers, laughed and continued about their business. Why? It wasn't even that they didn't want any trouble from the officers, because I knew their past records. So I asked them, Why did they let it slide? And one stated, "The shit is played out, it's so old the shit is funny! Straight up. How many white brothas and Latinos do we have calling each other nigga! So when an ignorant mutha fucka like him calls one of us a **nigger**, it ain't got shit to do with us no more. It's like a strike against his slow, stupid ass." Then another man replied, "When people feel inferior to a situation they lash out. It's like arguing with your woman; you gonna say shit to get under her skin, if it don't work you gonna be like, damn, what do I do next? As long as he don't put his hands on me, because then I'm gonna have to beat his ass!" The second incident in the penitentiary happened on "yard" and concerned the weight bench. Both black and white men claimed that it was their turn to go next, an argument ensued, and the N word was said to the brotha out of hate. The brotha took his turn anyway, laughing, and no punches were thrown! Again, I later asked why he let it slide, and he said, "Because that shit sounds corny now. It's like still putting cheese on a mousetrap when the mouse is wise to the catch! I could easily beat his ass, but it makes me feel better to watch him squirm, wondering why the hell I let it slide. It's like he's out of ammunition." With literally hundreds and hundreds of times every day in the penitentiary where the N word is said by all races, without malice, those were the only two times within two years that I witnessed negativity—and of all places, we were in the penitentiary, where you'd expect the opposite!

After release, I was out for a whole year before I heard the N word again being used in a negative way, inside a lounge. It was between a white army sergeant and a black navy officer. The black man spilled the white man's drink, and although he apologized, he was called the N word. The same laugh came from the brotha as he walked away. Why? So I asked him. "Because none of my white friends would have said such a thing. I had to catch myself from a negative response, because I'm not a loser."

So, in both situations, the script has been flipped, whereas in the '90s the N word would have caused an instant fight. Being incarcerated with people of so many nationalities saying the word nigga let me truly see how perceptions have changed for so many lives due to street culture. How long can mainstream society put off such an intricate and powerful element as the street culture? Not just the N word, but everything that represents the literal life.

If you cannot understand a brotha calling his white friend nigga, or vice versa, then it only shows the bridge between street ethics and what is believed to be society's moral ethics. After reading this, there will still be many whites who feel no need to say the N word, as well as some who would like to, because they feel close to their black friends and are definitely not saying it in a negative way. There will be blacks who don't feel the need to say it, as there are blacks who constantly say the N word, as well as call their close friends the N word. The new era of people will know when to say it, and how to say it. (Again, this is shedding light on what is factually happening; you'll have to decide where you fit in.)

Here's what we're up against. General society doesn't hear about the N word until there's a touchy issue where certain organizations bring it to the media's attention. Therefore, general society is unaware of how much the N word is actually being used—by all. Is it wrong? Who's to say? Is it professional blacks who feel they represent the street entity fighting against it? And when going public about this so-called negative N word, isn't it moral gratification, apology, and affirmation we seek? Aren't we getting more than that with the negativity being washed away by this new concept that blacks themselves have created? Isn't it worth something that the younger generation has a different concept of an old hate word? Isn't that what society and life is all about—progression? And though Martin Luther King Jr. wouldn't use the word himself, (because of the times) wouldn't he seriously analyze the ironic concept switch from negative to positive and see the intent of the younger generation; presently (of all races)? And wouldn't Malcolm X smirk with satisfaction to know that his people ingeniously turned the tables and took over the deed to the house—by all means necessary?

In the end, it all revolves around perception. Your perception is personal and unique, because how we view America and what we do in America creates America. Society tends to follow the perception of masses—what's supposedly the majority. If the majority finally realizes that an old issue is not as big as it once was, people can move ahead. It's time to move ahead. Choosing not to use the N word is a personal choice, but the more you hear it being said, don't cringe. Simply understand that it does have a new use and concept to many on the street. It's like cursing; none of us are supposed to do it, and yet everyone does!

(PERSONAL RESPECT)

"I got the spot for you! If you could make it there, you could make it anywhere! You'll be walking in the lion's den," said my friend Greg, expressing his skepticism about a club called the Green Mill where he was trying to get me to perform.

"They're all white-collar business people, getting off work and unwinding," he went on, while frantically pulling on a cigarette. "And they're hard, they're real hard. They'll probably boo you off the stage, but it will be good exposure for you. I'll let people know that you're there with me, maybe they'll be easy on you." I thanked him, but told him that wouldn't be necessary. However, he could still come if he wanted.

The Green Mill on Sunday nights hosted a SLAM competition. SLAM is a new style of poetry, quite flamboyant and sporadic, where you have an option of a jazz band backing you up. Judges grade you on your material, and if your shit is weak the crowd can boo you off the stage. It's a mixture of the Apollo, *Star Search*, and a poetry reading. The problem is that with different areas comes a different crowd, and with a different crowd comes a different understanding of poetry. But I couldn't wait because these were the challenges I lived for.

Sunday came and I took two of my best supporters, Mary and Journae. (I had to plead with one of the only four black people in the club to use his I.D. so that Journae could get in—he wasn't twenty-one yet.) Mark Smith was the host MC and did about three SLAMS before the competition started. I remembered seeing him on a *Dateline* segment on SLAM.

Four people went before me. As I watched the crowd's response, I noticed that they were stern, but fair. One couple got booed off stage, but they deserved it. They didn't have their act together and kept laughing at each other.

Then Mark Smith called me. "And now, ladies and gentlemen, we have a treat for you. We have K-So from Cabrini Green!" The crowd applauded and some looked puzzled, as if they felt that no one from Cabrini "fit in" at this establishment. At least that's how I perceived it. As I walked on stage, I heard one lady cry out, "Is he really from Cabrini?" Although this added to my concern about if they'd have any respect for me, it made me grab the mic with even more flair. It was my time to take over the joint. Like a volcano erupting, I did my thing. Not only was the respect they were giving evident, but they wanted to know more, hanging on my every word. Feeling me.

When I was almost done, I saw my friend Greg coming through the front door, late. I finished my SLAM with a roar and the crowd jumped up cheering with a standing ovation! Greg couldn't believe it as he looked around. While I walked off the stage, people were hollering, "Encore!"

As the night went on, my score was unmatched and I ended up winning first place. The crowd insisted I do another piece. I did.

The way we perceive people, sometimes by past experiences, what we've seen or heard blocks our positive balance with the way we feel toward them. Thus, it's hard to have respect for them because we feel they have no respect for us. It's basically tick for tack, which ruins anything that could have been positive. Had I gone into the Green Mill with anger at this yuppie crowd, maybe I would have been booed off stage because I would have already been set up for a downfall. They'd a been able to sense my aura.

However, the Green Mill showed me respect. They listened first before deciding, respecting my delivery, lifestyle, and message. I know for a fact that what I delivered was something they weren't used to, but they decided (out of respect) to absorb it.

To me, respect means sometimes listening, sometimes learning, sometimes crying, sometimes praying, often sharing, and sometimes being humble; to hold someone in high regard, either because of what they've been through, their accomplishments, or their plight, to give them credit.

Afterward, people gave me pamphlets, cards, numbers, handshakes, and hugs. We drove Greg home. Along the way he was quiet, and to me seemed jealous. I was disappointed in him, because as far as I was concerned, it was a triumph for both of us. I felt proud when I saw him come through the door, even being late.

The Green Mill had shown me all the respect in the world. Greg, on the contrary, had shown me no respect at all.

(WHO'S TEXT?)

There was a cell phone text message that circulated around Halloween for three years in a row. I thought the text was funny and sent it to a bunch of my friends. The short text read as follows:

A black baby was given wings by God.
The baby asked, "Does this mean I'm an Angel?"
God laughed and said, "Naw, nigga, you a bat!"
Happy Halloween.

When I sent this to a bunch of my friends, everyone replied how funny it was—all but one person. What I had forgotten was that, as I sent it out simultaneously, I hadn't determined by race who received it—because I don't view my friends as such. The one person who eventually didn't think it was funny was a white gentleman named Terry. At first, Terry really liked it, and because he truly thought it was funny, he passed it along. That was when the trouble began. What he assumed was funny was not perceived as such by many of his friends—simply because he was white.

Terry called me and said, "Man, K, that text got me in some hot water! People who I thought would think it was funny started trippin'. Black **and** white. This one lady texted me back, asking me what the hell I was talking about. And this one brotha told me not to text him shit like that anymore. What did I do wrong? I'm not on no racial stuff." I sighed and told him that it would probably be best if he stopped texting it to people.

This sunk into my mind for a moment, how people view things so differently. A joke can be perceived as taboo by races simply by the person telling it, or by one word. In this case, both the word **nigga** and Terry's race played a part. If just that one word, **nigga**, would have been replaced by **brotha**, then it wouldn't have been as racial. And the rest would have fallen on Terry and how he was perceived by the race of those he'd sent it to.

As I mentioned earlier, in the "N word" segment, we are at a critical point in history where moving ahead as a people is strictly based upon perception; and more so the importance of the outcome, than the initial perception itself.

In Terry's case, **respect** would have been better off as a two-way street. Those that he'd texted the joke to should have had the respect as Terry's friends to realize that it was simply a Halloween text joke, and not based it on the color of his skin. And Terry, respecting his friends, should have sent it to only those whom he was sure would not be offended.

Many times, racial perceptions are attacked with humor, and this is probably the most powerful incentive we currently produce. One perfect example of this would be the Dave Chapelle show. Though he is no longer running it, it would be of importance to catch some of his past material. We are currently at a stage where humor coats the sharp sting of what we perceive to be problematic.

Claiming a scenario automatically pits people against one another—so whose text is it? The sender or the recipient? The race that is the butt of the joke, or the race laughing at the joke? Or does the joke become alive itself, perceived differently by all?

Respect ties into the fabric of reasoning and understanding
K-SO G (2007).

MIXED COUPLES

Inter-ra-cial (in-ter-ray-shal) adj. For, of, among, or between races or people of different races.

Interracial couples. Yes, say it again! The word "interracial" should be embedded in gold stone! Interracial couples should be looked upon as diamonds, platinum, or the big lottery! Lately, we as Americans have looked upon the word "interracial" as taboo, only mentioning it when we have to and feeling slightly awkward when we use the word. What a weak way to tackle the subject! In fact, interracial couples have the invisible power that we as a nation need to tap into. These are the exact people who have shown us what being real is all about. "Interracial" should be an honored word because it shows that a couple has decided be trendsetters in a world that needs them. Going back to what I was saying about visual effects, interracial couples have taken the first step in proving that not only have they survived the visual effect, but they are on a whole other level.

Though interracial is a blessed word, let's face it, it's long and it sounds proper, as though it is the educated way to state something. It's quite formal. So from here on in (more so on the regular, everyday speaking level), we will address interracial couples as "mixed couples." It's down-to-earth, easy, to the point, and valid. This also goes for men, women, and children who are conceived interracially—we'll simply say "mixed."

We live in a world that needs pioneers to effect change, yet it still doesn't come easy. These so-called pioneers are basically those who do what they feel is right, regardless of others, and if a concept gets slowly adopted by the mainstream, followers give it a try. How can we be this docile? Why does the American public wait for others to pioneer a basic concept that need not be thought of as an issue? It's important for the American public to view mixed dating as the positive factor that it is. You are taking two people and they are not only learning about a relationship in this hard world, but about each other. And what they learn (mostly positive aspects) is passed along.

Society implies that it's okay to date interracially, they bash racist talk shows, the news talks coldly of hate crimes, and the press attacks the prejudiced. But in doing so, the news and media subliminally glorify the existence of hate—it's news, so much so and by so many angles that it awkwardly seems interesting to the weak-minded. They exploit it so much that the issue itself becomes taboo, to the point you don't even talk about it, you just watch and listen to others talk about it and don't want to be bothered with it. Thus, this becomes your perception of anything racial. To see a mixed couple, the first thing you think is, "Wow! They have guts." So, although society says it's okay, you know that they're implying it's "supposed to be" okay.

When mixed couples walk down the street, there are two angles that need to be talked about. The first angle is from the mixed couple's point of view. We already realize that you're strong people because you're trendsetters, so I'm going to describe a few scenes that you'll be able to relate to:

1. When walking down the street, it seems that people may be staring at you, and that's because they are.
2. When dining in a restaurant, you might catch someone nonchalantly watching you as you eat.
3. While pulling through a drive through, the cashier looks at you and your date and smiles, being extra-polite and giving you extra condiments!
4. If you have kids and you're walking through the park as a family, people look at you, then at your spouse, then at your kids, and smile.

Now from the observer's point of view, on the same four incidents. Remember, since society has pummeled you with cluttered ideas of how people view you, it's important to stay focused. Ninety percent of people (as I said) think that you have guts, and applaud your leadership and diversity. It not as big as we've all made it and you need to be reminded of that.

1. When walking down the street, people notice new things while out and about. Since mixed couples are still fresh in society's eyes, of course people notice you. So what! You're fresh and inspiring; you have a flair about your chemistry.

Elders notice you because they remember a time when it was beyond rare to see a mixed couple, especially in public; black men notice other black men who are dating a white woman (Latino, Filipino, etc.), because they're paying attention to how he's dressed, his speech, his movements, and how presentable she looks.

The same thing with white men; they notice other white men who are with black women. Many white men think black women are attractive, they just aren't sure about from what angle to approach them. So, when they see a white man with a black woman, they're paying close attention to the chemistry, his clothing, his speech, and how he treats his female. You also have to remember that there will be different scales of mixed couples. For example: Young white street guys may date only young black street girls, who have a certain style of clothing, speech, music, and ideas of fun; the same with upper-class black women who will only date corporate white men. In each instance, it's still white males dating black females, just on different levels of the economic ladder, bringing along different options of interest.

So the next time you're walking down the street, think about both angles. If you're a leader, don't worry about the stares. You're just a hot commodity with interesting viewpoints. If you're an observer, just show a little respect and try not to stare—it kinda makes you look lonely.

2. Everybody says they don't have trouble eating in front of a date, but somewhere along the line they do. It's just normal. So, when you're at a restaurant and it seems that people are hawking you a little, remember three things:

   A. They're slightly uncomfortable with the situation at their own table and are looking for a scapegoat, so they look away from their date and just notice you because you stand out slightly and are interesting.

B. A lot of times (and we do this ourselves), we look at something and our minds are focused on something else. So, being a mixed couple, you may have caught his or her attention and he or she started to reminisce on a former experience with someone of another race. Often people catch themselves when they realize they've stared too long. Though it may seem that they're staring at you, their focus is somewhere else.

C. As I said before, 90 percent of the time people admire your courage and think it's truly pleasant seeing a mixed couple. Show them that you're having a good time and often you won't even notice the stares.

3. Remember, you are trendsetters in this dog-eat-dog world! When you pull into a drive through, the focus is on serving you. The cashier has been serving people all day; she's tired and cranky; people have come through with attitudes and she's ready to go home. But as she sees the two of you pull up, it's refreshing to her eyes because it's human nature to applaud achievement. The positive energy you produce attracts attention, and in her own way she's adding to your energy slightly in the things she does. If it's a nice smile (the first and last of the day) with some extra condiments, so be it.

4. Families that stay together are already a great asset to humanity, so mixed couples that stand the test of time, with children, are survivalists. How can anyone (young, old, racist or humanitarian) not notice such a vibrant family? If a mixed couple is walking through the park with children, it's a powerful statement of self. The smiles you receive are reflections of your own achievement.

The bottom line is that things are not as big as they seem to be. Don't let observers throw you off your square; you've already mentally won. A punk will only say something to you because you've broken his perception of life; you've made your own rules and he can't relate. It's a shame that people should waste such energy, but they do—so beat his ass! No, just kidding, simply laugh at his or her ignorance because he or she are losers in life. You just continue moving ahead.

(WOMEN WHO'VE NEVER DATED OUT OF THEIR RACE)

Women (white or black) aren't saying they wouldn't date out of their race, they're just saying that they don't feel that they have to, because thus far it hasn't presented itself as an option. And oftentimes, how can it? If you're a black female on the South Side of Chicago, Harlem, or Watts, for miles around all you have is other blacks. Even if you work downtown around all whites, this field of whites may seem rigid, intimidating, or strict because they're not what you're looking for. Thus, your perception of white men is basically what you've encountered.

Some white women, whether or not they want to admit it, feel that getting serious with a black man would be unrealistic. They may be okay in sports, but as far as raising a family, thinking clearly, and being stable, it's just too far-fetched.

Every now and then, an occasion arises on either side (black or white) where you encounter someone with whom you are truly compatible. This encounter happens so suddenly that, although in your heart you may feel this person is perfect for you, somehow you mismanage the moment. And before you know it, the person is gone—no exchange of numbers or future plans, simply gone. After this happens, you often think of this person, wondering "what if." This too can be a disappointment that furthers your distance from another race, simply by giving up.

There are some pro-black women who won't date out of their race and try to get others to do the same. I think that's fine if you allow yourself to feel this way, but let others decide for themselves, on their own balance of life. You can't speak for all African Americans; it belittles the race and makes it seem like your judgment speaks for everyone. It's like the KKK producing a speech and feeling representative of all whites, when they're not.

Women have a lot to fight for in America with equal rights. As a woman, you're faced with the overwhelming hurdle—meaning, you're going to have to jump higher than others to be noticed equally. With that in mind, don't close options to self-balance. Sometimes life can give the extra balance you need through a person, someone you never thought possible. If you're a woman, whether pro-black, Irish, or Spanish, ask yourself: What are the best qualities of being loved? What gives substance to a dreary life? And most of all, isn't it your right as a citizen on this planet to be happy?

I'm not saying dump your boyfriend, change your beliefs, or quit being militant. I'm simply saying keep your mind open to the future; the best encounter may still be yet to come.

(GAY AND LESBIAN COUPLES)

People don't know this, but there's a serious struggle in the gay community with mixed couples—not so much with the mixed couple itself, but the background and the values of the race. Gays have to realize that it's going to be harder for your community because gay rights aren't fully respected in society, and then you're having these side issues with race relations within your community! The bottom line is this, you guys: You should be the first group of people to get over this racial barrier, and sadly you aren't. I'm disappointed in the gay community for not trying harder to tackle these issues. It shows that things are still about money, race, and politics, even within the gay community. But I have to say that there are many affluent, professional, and solid mixed couples in the gay community that are doing wonders for your cause. Study them, meet them, and network with them; they are men and women of true balance and an asset to your plight.

Lesbian women have found more of a balance than gay men in mixed couples. This is a good tool within the lesbian community, because women sadly have more to prove in America than men, and with mixed couples comes balance and with balance comes strength. To all you "butches" or "studs" (the dominant partner in a female relationship; however, the term currently popular with the younger lesbians is "stud") out there, if you're in a mixed couple relationship, don't let your dominance speak for your race, especially if you're overprotective, mentally abusive, or violent. This disintegrates the positive balance that you two have and ruins her perception of what you used to represent. I'd like to say that lesbians have a powerful voice in America right now, and mixed lesbian couples are noticed even more, so the two together offers a voice that America will have to recognize as a power to be reckoned with. Look out, future.

(WHY IT'S SO IMPORTANT)

When Malcolm X wrote from Mecca, he discussed a true brotherhood between his Muslim brethren. Men with blond hair and blue eyes who welcomed him as family, eating from the same bowl and drinking from the same cup, who would gladly lay down their lives for him and Allah in a heartbeat. He came back to America with a new understanding of race relations. Though he finally severed his ties with Elijah Muhammad, (it was believed that Elijah was behind Malcolm's murder). Malcolm had given his life for his belief and died an honored man.

In 1968, when Martin Luther King Jr. was assassinated, my mother was on Chicago's outer drive heading home. As the announcement came over the car radio, she pulled over to the shoulder lane, parked, and wept aloud. This was the effect Dr. King had on just about all of America. An incredible man with the will to love during the heat of attack. A man who actually had a vision through a dream that spoke of what appeared to be the future. During this time of water hoses, dog bites, and racial tension, he boldly said, "I refuse to let you bring me down," and kept on marching. This let society know that they had a true leader at hand. How could anyone belittle themselves to criticize his deep dedication to what he believed in? He was a man of principle, honor, and determination. And he, too, gave his life for his cause.

I often sit back and wonder how much of a life can a man have if he's chasing a truth that people aren't ready for? If you're chasing a dream that no one else has witnessed? Yet you make people feel you and see what you see through your motivation to reach, your determination to surpass, and your will to express. Could you imagine living a life where you have no life, because you're on the road trying to change everybody else's? What nobility.

Why is death the ultimate standoff with hate? I still sit back and wonder about that. But more so, I think about the future and the deaths to come. Not because we finally got over this racial barrier, but because we didn't. Listen, in the years to come, the issue of mixed couples will get less and less attention because it will be so common. People need people for love, comfort, intimacy, happiness, and inspiration. So, if you let people stop you from the inevitable, then you are weaker than our forefathers who thought the world was flat. So the next time you hear the word "interracial," remember that it's a blessed word. A mixed couple is a blessed couple! Believe that.

HIP HOP B-BOP DON'T STOP?

(Always)

In May of 1983, I turned off the radio, and me and two of my partners counted our money. At thirteen, I had made four hundred and forty-four dollars from five hours of work, break dancing in front of the **Water Tower**.

It was seven o'clock at night and only half the fun had been achieved in my day. Now it was time to "test the city," as we called it, because the practice part of my day was over.

One of my partners was a female named Toni, who was better at **poplocking, ticking,** and **animation** than any guy who stepped to her. Point-blank. My other partner, Ronnie, had the **footwork, pennies,** and **tabletops down packed.** And I was a combination of the two, with one added touch.

From competing in gymnastics when I was younger, I incorporated the "Thomas Flares" into my break dancing. This was a skill that Olympic medalist Kurt Thomas used to do on the pommel horse. Mine would be on the bare ground, and were the freshest flares in the Windy City! Yeah, I'm bragging. But how's this for size: years later, a mutual friend let me hear an old tape from a hot underground Chicago rapper. There was this one line that said:

"My lyrics make you pass that B, cuz you know you gotta share,
"Make you say damn! Like the Pete Keller Flares!"

So I suppose I made my mark. Then about a year after that, I was at UMOJA (a yearly festival held by Cabrini) and a rapper got on stage and said a similar line about my flares. I was speechless. After he performed, he got lost in the crowd and I couldn't find him. For those who don't know, my name is Pete Keller; I didn't give myself the name K-So G until I was thirteen, and it stands for **Knowledge, Survival, Opportunity, and Guidance.**

Toni and I rolled up the linoleum while Ronnie split the money and handed it to us. We grabbed the radio, hit the train, and were on our way to Sox Park. There was a game that night.

On the train ride we rapped, collected more money, and had people clapping. We got off on 35ᵗʰ and pushed our way through the blocked-off streets. People were everywhere, and I noticed how beat-up and tired the old Comisky Park looked.

We had a slick routine (we call this a **cap move**) that we took citywide. This is what we'd do: since the radio attracted attention in any neighborhood we'd go to, we always had Toni walk two blocks behind us when it was time for action. She'd watch with the crowd. Always. Ronnie would bust some phony moves, but good enough just to catch bait, and I would talk shit, backing him up and waiting for a catch. "Yo, that's fresh! Man, Ron, dog, you got the moves! I bet nobody out here can fade that." And someone would always come forth. Always.

With break dancing, it's always about showing your moves, because you've practiced them at home and in your neighborhood, and can't wait to show them off, especially if someone from another neighborhood came through and their shit was whack. And that was us—or so they thought.

"Yo! Me and my guy right here could fade that shit. What's up, wanna battle?" came a voice from the crowd. Ronnie, Toni, and I eyeballed each other; we'd already won, but it was time for action.

I turned up the volume on the radio as our competitors bust out a nice routine in sync. The crowd went wild (in break dancing, the crowd always judged; it didn't matter what type of neighborhood, the crowd was always fair—always), and after they finished I hollered over the radio, "Damn, you guys are better. You wanna put some money up? I got a hundred-dollar bill says me and my guy can beat you! In fact, I'll even pick someone out the crowd to join us and we'll still beat you." It was an offer they couldn't refuse. Because for one, we were in "their" neighborhood, and two, in quickly glancing at the crowd, they were looking for guys, not girls. So, since they knew the guys in their neighborhood who could break, they weren't worried, and accepted the challenge, gladly. Sometimes they didn't have the whole hundred between the two or three of them (or however many there were), but we wouldn't take less than fifty! The money was always given to a female in the front and she was placed next to the radio (sometimes she would hold the radio so we could watch her).

"Ya bet. Here goes our hundred, right here," one of the guys said, handing it to a female I had chosen. I gave her our hundred and Ronnie and I snapped out on a routine. The crowd was ecstatic! Our opponents looked at each other, somewhat realizing they'd been played, so they frantically bust out their best shit and called for back up. "Hey, someone go get Ray Ray. Hurry up! He's over there, working the parking lot." We didn't care who the hell they got, that's what Toni was for, our hidden ammo.

Ray Ray came running over and the crowd parted, letting him through. But it didn't matter, he was no match for Ronnie and me. The crowd couldn't wait for us to go again. Our shit was together, the moves were precise, and most of all, we were having fun. Real fun! Routine after routine, Ronnie and I bust out until not only had they given up, but you could tell they were biting our moves. I then waved for Toni to come out, and the crowd was in such a frenzy that you could barely hear the music. I could tell by the way all the females were fixed on Toni's every move that they idolized her more than Janet Jackson, and all the guys were simply in love.

We'd literally pulled half of the outside White Sox crowd, everyone wanting to see what was going on. Crowds draw crowds, especially when they see people jumping up and down, clapping and cheering.

We played people in **Breakin'** as many get played in basketball, and it was fair because you accepted the challenge.

We cut off the music, grabbed the money (I gave the girl who was holding the money five bucks, she was a cutie-pie), and exchanged info with the other breakers. This was the law of the land, you always networked. And this is how it went down everywhere we went. We were prepared, we practiced, and we had tricks up our sleeves—and we always collected our money. Always.

(Chicago Hip Hop)

Chicago embraced Hip Hop as New York once had. It was a component and street concept that allowed you to go anywhere in the city, despite the gangs. Yes! People will never realize how amazing this was. Because at first, break dancing was as much hip hop as hip hop itself. From 1983 to 1986, break dancing lived in Chicago and was at its peak. In 1986, it slowly faded out and **Mcing** (rapping, including rap "mc" battles) took over—not to mention gangbanging once again took priority.

Chicago will never realize how important those three years were in our city's history. The difference between New York and Chicago was that New York created Hip Hop as a supplement for the gang activity that basically stopped overnight because of it. Chicago embraced Hip Hop as a trend that allowed you to be separated temporarily from the gangs, but eventually couldn't compete with the diversity of the city. But while it was in swing, man, it was love!

During 1968, when Dr Martin Luther King Jr. died, all the city gangs came to an agreement that there would be peace for a whole week in remembrance. You could go anywhere on any turf that you normally couldn't. Well, this is what happened for three years straight when **Breakin'** was alive and well in Chicago. I often wish my kids could have seen this; I wish the youth of today could understand the power this art form carried.

As break dancing competitions swept the city all neighborhoods welcomed others in artistic rivalry. The best crews with the best styles won and were honored. **Latin Kings** could go into **Latin Eagles'** neighborhoods, compete, leave untouched, and be shooting at each other that night. If you were a **Gangster Disciple**, you could go into a **Blackstone** neighborhood, battle, and breakout, untouched! This shit was happening and people didn't realize what the hell they had in front of them.

Breakin' battles were everywhere, and along with them came the other four components: **DJing, Mcing** (Rappin' and beat boxin'), **Graffitti**, and **Hip-hop Fashion** (styles, clothing, and slang). Graffiti crews popped up everywhere. The name of my crew was **F.I.C.** (Fresh Image Crew, then later First In Control—my tag was "Frosty"). In the circle of Hip Hop, your aim was to try and do it all the best you could. Your goal was to be "all around" in all five components.

Some of the pioneer Chicago all-city" writing crews were: TCP, FIC, ABC, CTA, GGC, Feds, PIC, WAR, LONS, OTR, and MOSA.

Some gave their lives during this time, such as KRE 8, Pilot, and HATE 1. It was a time in Chicago when parties were open to anyone. You could literally walk off the street into most parties; gangbanging was put to the side temporarily for these three years.

There was another struggle going on during this period in Chicago. It was Hip Hop vs. House, and it was all-out war. A confused war. Hip Hop came to Chicago during a time when House music was all that Chicago was about. Period. We were the capital of the world in House music, and still continue to be. And I'm not talking about the old deep house music, where there's a lot of singing and instruments (that too will always be strong here, though), I'm talking about straight-up beats, bass beats that were over 110 RPMs. This was the straight-up shit that we lived for (staying up late at night to record the Hot Mix Five on **wbmx**), which was basically a cousin to hip hop, simply sped up. Man, I'm talking that the House music back then (it was about a three-year period, around the same time as the Breakin') consisted of the coldest beats I've heard to this day; strictly beats, and everybody knew them, as if they were a single song, but in actuality it was! You should have seen the dance floor. As soon as a particular House beat came on, everybody knew it and jumped up, crowding the dance floor. "Oh, snap! That's my shit!" people would scream. And this is what hip hop suddenly had to compete with. Also, you have to remember that rap at this point was not considered hip hop, as it is now. Although it was a component of hip hop, it was still new, and since hip hop hadn't really invaded Chicago yet, it was separated from Hip Hop and was simply looked upon as Rap music. Which was interesting to us, but there was no way in hell we were going to dance to it. We couldn't. We literally could not dance to rap music at that time in Chicago. We were all about House. That's all we knew, that's all our dances went to. When the integrating popped up every now and then, with the DJ throwing on a rap record, this was our break time, bathroom time, go check on the car time! So, as our first hip hoppers embraced the culture, many of them pledged "Hip Hop or nothing," which meant House was not acceptable, an enemy—a **no-no**. However, I could not accept this ideology, and wherever my hip hop following directed me I let them know! First, I've got too much pride in Chicago, and the fact that we pioneered House and its ever-changing style, just like hip hop. Second, man, music is music. When our first pioneers of Hip Hop in Chicago said "Hip Hop or nothing," they still listened to slow cuts, they still listened to Dusty's. And believe me, they were probably sneaking a listen to House because it was just too hot back then. You had Frankie Knuckles, Farley Jack master Funk, Scott Smokin' Seals, Adonis, Keith Nunley (J.M. Silk), Ten City, Mike Hitman Wilson, Ron Hardy, Jamie Principle, Mike Dunn, Fast Eddie, Ralphy the Razz Rosario, Steve Silk Hurley, Gene Hunt, and Kenny Jammin' Jason—and so many other raw underground badass DJ's! And third, I was young, going to all these fresh-ass house clubs and underground house parties, having the time of my life. I knew the DJ, I knew the people, so why couldn't I do both?

One thing we all had, though, was a deep respect and love for Hip Hop. We respected its founders, did our homework, and went by all the invisible laws and policies that came along with it. We realized Hip Hop came from New York and respected that. We had our share of battles with them, but it was all in the love of the sport. That's why the whole East Coast vs. West Coast thing blew us later on, because how can you disrespect the founders that opened the door for you to make money in the first place?

As time went on, Chicago had too many other interests: the adrenaline for gangbanging reclaimed, drugs (crack) came overnight to the youth, music changed (we even had a period of **Hip House**, which somewhat successfully brought the two together), people got older, and Hip Hop spread nationwide as a fad. There will always be those diehard Hip Hop fans in Chicago and abroad that hold on to those five components of Hip Hop. But I will always remember a time in Chicago that was like no other, a time when Hip Hop meant something, when youth throughout the city traveled to meet and express their art, to exchange pieces and drawing styles, clothes, numbers, moves, stories, and smiles. It was a time when a perfect non-adult yet positive force brought all youth together, who by no means or circumstances would have met otherwise. It was three magical years in Chicago that I wish we could regain, and then take nationwide.

(Words with Meaning)

Pay attention to Hip Hop words. Though we relate **Rap** to Hip Hop, it is not, and it is important to understand that though rap artists use a majority of the Hip Hop terms, it is Hip Hop that created these words—and not rap. It is also important to remember that a majority of rap (nationwide) is not **gangster** rap; it just isn't: There's storytelling, political, love ballads, conscious, battle rhyming, and party raps. So even when hardcore—gangster—rappers use common rap words, they still are coming from the overall rap community that got them from the Hip-hop community; thus not representative of what appears to be **only** the gangster rap community. For instance, from the mid '80s through the '90s, the word **Peace** was used in the Hip-hop community, which rappers immediately appropriated, using it at the end of their raps. It immediately caught on nationwide, as it had a decade earlier with the '70s Woodstock era.

During the end of the '90s, a new word hit the scene—**One**. This word replaced **Peace** with the same intent; an ending (farewell) note. What's interesting about both **One** and **Peace** are the powerful meanings! The word **Peace** is a universal hope, such as **world peace**, with the intent of all getting along. With the word **One**, the implication is All Being One—we are together, as one! Damn, in an all too diverse rap arena, with the majority of America (commercial America) feeling that gangster rap represents Hip Hop, how do these words cling to what appears to be negative? Well, it's quite simple. Remember, Hip Hop is the majority culture, not rap. And Hip Hop is the developmental source of creating words, not rap—and Hip Hop is positive! Thus, the trickle-down effect moves from its source to its components. Hip Hop is creativity, and creativity comes from self, and mans true self is positive. Period.

(Hip-hop Tops)

Since Hip Hop is an issue that has grown with America over the last twenty years, I often wonder how others feel about it. Usually, when I'm with someone in that arena—celebrity, political figure, or complete stranger—I ask them questions pertaining to the future of Hip Hop. Here are some short statements.

Out of breath from doing a rap for Rev. Jesse Jackson, he hugged me and I went up to bat:

- **K**: Jesse, do you think Hip Hop has a political voice?
- **Jesse**: Yes. Yes, very much so. The young people of today have a voice and it needs to be heard…and those that grew up on it are adults now, and their voice is already being heard!
- Old-school Funkadelic **George Clinton** (of the Parliaments) was at the studio with me last year. While taking a food break, he said, "You know, Hip Hop is changing. I hope I'm here to see where it ends up going. You guys, especially you, are going to be the ones to take it to a new level. The voice is so strong, with worldwide influence; you have got to take advantage of it."
- Outside the corner liquor store in Cabrini Green stands fifty-two-year-old **Gus**. He's there from sunup to sundown.
- **K**: What's up, Gus, you sly dog, you? Hey, Gus, you always reading the papers out here and singing someone's rap song. What do you think is going to happen to Hip Hop in the years to come?
- **Gus**: Well, I know one thing, I seen enough of y'all spinning on y'alls head and shit! Remember that, boy? You used to rip up all ya clothes…Well, if Hip Hop is gonna live, you young folk gotta do some new shit because everything gets old after a while. First they had the bellbottoms on the bottom, then they had the bell bottoms on the top, when they called it baggies. I'm telling you what they gonna do next; they gonna take that shit to the middle, and have bell bottoms on the knees. Watch! Now, I answered your question, boy, give me a dollar on this Richards!
- Last year I wrote a rap for actor **Todd Bridges** (**"Willis"** from *Different Strokes*). We had a good time in the studio, he's a good person. This was his reply on the future of Hip Hop.

- **Todd**: In the years to come, Hip Hop is going to change because the style in America itself is changing, on everything. It's deep, but I'm sure Hip Hop will evolve with it.
- I brought rapper **Fat Joe** and his posse to Cabrini, and as we took pictures and kicked it, I brought it up.
- **K**: Let's get down to it, Joe. What does Hip Hop mean to you?
- **Joe**: Man, it's like a whole culture…a way of living. Those that didn't grow up on it are finally starting to learn about it, and it's blowing up. Just watch what's to come. Watch. Just watch!
- I was backstage with **Willie D** (of the **Ghetto Boys**) and he put one of my shorty rappers on the spot.
- **Willie D**: I heard you can rap. Go ahead and bust something.
- **K**: My shorty froze up, so I smacked him on the back of his neck—hard. "Boy, that's Willie D! Don't play with me, you better brainstorm or something!" Embarrassed, he did his rap, all smiles. After he was done, I asked Willie D what direction he felt Hip Hop was going to take, not rap.
- **Willie D**: Well, Hip Hop is deeper than people think because there's so many styles to it, and it brings people together. I don't know what specific direction it's going to take, but I know it's going to be a positive one.
- I met **Beth**, a homeless white woman on Lower East Wacker Drive. She was lying on top of newspaper, doing a crossword book had she found. After finding out a little about her, I asked.
- **K**: Beth, what do you think about Hip Hop? Do you think it's going to do anything positive in the future for the younger generation?
- **Beth**: Well, it doesn't seem like it has a political forum. I can't see it going too far. It's mostly music now, it seems to me. My son used to be involved when break dancing was big, but now he's into real estate…I guess he grew out of it. Forget him. He's an asshole anyway. (After a couple of hours talking with Beth, I sadly heard about her trouble with drugs. I gave her a couple of numbers to call. I pray that she decided to do so.)
- I keep bumping into **Jermaine Dupri**. The last time I saw him was at the New Music Seminar, so I asked.

- **K**: Jermaine, you've been doing your thing for a minute now. Do you think Hip Hop could die out just like that?

- **Jermaine**: No, because of one reason. People like me and you won't let it!

- I ran into rapper/actor **Ice T** at the Players Ball and asked.

- **K**: What's up, big ole pimp? Man, why hasn't Hip Hop died out?

- **Ice T**: Because, K-So, as you know, there's money in organization. Whenever you have something that can reproduce sales off its fashion, music, or whatever, then you have something that's valuable. What I want to see is how valuable it will be when it's taken to a level where we control the money.

- I met **Afrika Bambatta** (Hip-hop legend, pioneer, and leader of the **Zulu Nation**) at Rainbo's Zulu Nation party.

- **K**: So, how does it feel to see everything fall into place with your vision of Hip Hop?

- **Bam**: We're always trying to expand further, but it's good to see it spread to these other cities. Hip Hop is here to stay; it's just the style that's going to change.

- While attending our monthly Naras meetings at the Excaliber, I pulled **Bernie Mack** to the side for an interview. After kicking it with him, I asked.

- **K**: Can you see advancement in Hip Hop, or decrease?

- **Bernie**: It's hard to say, because people look at it differently wherever you go. Folks in the suburbs don't give a damn, people in Wyoming probably don't know what it is…Is Hip Hop a new dance, peanut butter, or pogo stick!

- I briefly lamped with **Kid Rock** after a performance at the Double Door.

- **K**: Your talent with the instruments is tight. It's cold how you switch around like that. Do you see any switching around for the Hip Hop movement coming up?

- **Kid Rock**: Yeah, because everything is changing now. Our parents see that a lot of the things they taught us has nothing to do with how we're living now. We need something more solid that can hold us together as we change. It would be cool if it was Hip Hop.

- When **Nas** came to Cabrini (with **R. Kelly**) to shoot his Street Dreamers video, I grabbed my moment.
- **K**: Where do you see Hip Hop five years from now?
- **Nas**: As a tool for young children; something educational they can benefit from.
- Well last, but definitely not least, is my secret sweetheart MC Lyte. I'll never forget interviewing her backstage in her dressing room. It was so small that she had to sit on the makeup table, and I had to stand up (practically between her legs). We were so close that all I could think about was leaning over and giving her a passionate kiss!
- **K**: So now, for your final question. What's Hip Hop going to end up becoming?
- **Lyte**: Hip Hop is basically a household name now. Its job is to expand and get more respect. I see a lot of political avenues in the making. It can become what we make it.

So there you have it. And though I have many more Hip-hop interviews with major celebrities, I shan't bore you with those now. My point is that, through the different ways of putting it, basically all the answers said the same thing:

1. That there is a future for Hip Hop.
2. That Hip Hop is what we the people involved make it.
3. That it's a tool that can be used financially, motivationally, educationally, politically, and influentially.

This is serious and if these top artists and celebrities are coming to the same conclusion, then it's time to do something about it.

(Hip Hop, B-Bop, Don't Stop?)

To me, Hip Hop is alive and well in America, and yet it's not actually what I'm looking for anymore. I say anymore because to me, it's not the same.

Hip Hop used to be about life, about culture, about expression. It was your counselor to turn to when you needed encouragement. But then it became used like a Kleenex and thrown away. America got tired and simply moved on. And I'm not going to say white society, because that's not who it was. No. It was the press, news and media that exploited Hip Hop, hanging it out on the line to dry, jumping on the bandwagon like they do everything else and running it into the ground.

The reason I say it's alive and well is because how pure and raw it was. Although the news and media hurt it, it revived itself and continues to grow with the "Heads" of the new generation. The reason it will never be the same (or at least not until we do something about it) is because kids view Hip Hop as rap now, instead of the powerful culture it used to be. Rap is simply a component of Hip Hop.

As we get older, our lives become more serious with more responsibilities. What we need to do is find out how to incorporate Hip Hop into our lives, without walking away from its childishness. We need to organize Hip-hop leadership so that we can progress Hip Hop as a stepladder; meaning, different levels to adjust, acknowledge, administer, and comprehend; like there's a *Sports Illustrated* for kids and *Sports Illustrated* for adults.

When I say it's not what I'm looking for anymore, I mean just that. The stage (and state) where it is now and what it has become is not representative of what I know it's supposed to be; therefore, I can't look for something when I know it's been tampered with. I'll be down with the Hip-hop movement until the day I die, but it needs to progress. The Hip-hop B-Bop stuff is fine for our children, but we need more **Chuck Ds, Sista Souljas, Ice Ts, Queen Latifas, Afrika Bambattas**, and a political agenda (not just from rappers with a political conscience). We need political forums like Zulu Nation in every city. But we need it deeper than Hip Hop; we need political structure that is willing to follow through as a national voice. This will require time, leadership, participants, education (not so much in schooling, but in philanthropy), funding, and action. Thorough action. We are now talking about a progressive power with meaning and balance that any American can be proud to join. Just think about it; your child and you could belong to the same union, with the same goals! Hip Hop, B-Bop, Don't Stop? No, don't stop, just change—and in doing so, something else is going to have to change.

(ULON)

ULON (YU-LON) n. abbr. United Legion of One Nation. New term for old Hip-hop phrase.

During the late '70s and through the '90s, Hip Hop had five components: Break dancing, DJing, Mcing, Graffitti, and Fashion (terms, styles and clothes). When the year 2001 came, in a political forum by the movement, it was decided to add a sixth component, Political Agenda. Since this new component added a deeper overtone, concept, and plight, a more serious name was sought to represent the movement. The old term Hip Hop was changed to ULON, as people and organizations around the world embraced this new culture as the entity that it truly is.

Okay, Hip-hop world, movement, and artists! Get ready to hold on to your seats! on January 1, 2010, Hip Hop as we know it shall be no more! That's right! But don't trip! Simply the name...

Yes, we've grown now, and after twenty years, finally reaching the twenty-first century, we've got to push our Hip Hop heads into the political arena more and more. There are so many of us who are already there, but there's just one slight thing. Hip Hop is in desperate need of a new name. It's like the singing group Immature; once you get older, you outgrow a name like that. People know you and remember you from how you first started out. Hip Hop is more than twenty years old now, and it needs a new label that can carry it for the next one hundred years!

Our founding fathers will appreciate and respect this if they truly support the movement. A simple phrase should not hold us back.

Thousands of supporters have already called me, faxed, e-mailed, and written saying that we should have done this sooner. I take ULON (Hip Hop) seriously, and plan on contacting record companies, studios, newspapers, magazines, radio stations, other media, and promotion companies to let them know of "our" title change.

We're trying to stop our representatives from standing up in colleges, courts, or Congress and saying, "We're here on behalf of the hip-hop people." That's what they want, to make us look foolish. We are not to be taken as a joke, we are dead serious. Our youth has so much to offer and this is the best political forum to present it. That's why ULON is so important; it's the last thing we have that defines all of us, as one.

It's essential that we stop referring to ourselves (those over eighteen) as Hip Hop, because we've simply outgrown it. Let us embrace ULON as men and women of the twenty-first century.

Love and support,
K-So G

RUNNING

(Never Again)

When I was fourteen, I knew my way around Chicago like the back of my hand; the bus routes, train systems, and neighborhoods. In fact, I used to pride myself on just how many people I knew from each corner of the city, throughout, and in between. But there were always teens who knew more; teens who had come from different cities by themselves, drifting. These drifters (boys and girls) seemed to know so much. Stacey Nash was one of them.

I met Stacey when she was thirteen, at an open mic Hip-hop club called the Bedrock. (The upstairs was open to teens on Wednesday nights). She was about to grab the mic and rap, when our eyes met. Instantly, she grabbed my hand and pulled me onstage to rap with her, as if we were to do a duet, not even asking if I could rap. But I could, and we did, and as the crowd cheered us, I fell in love.

Stacey had run away from her father's custody in Washington, D.C. She hitchhiked everywhere she went, was not a virgin, and was so outgoing that during her three-week stay I left school every day at lunchtime to be with her. My parents didn't know, but Stacey came to live in my basement for her entire stay. I finally talked Stacey into going home. Whether she did or not, I'll never know—I never saw her again.

In 1986, I traveled to Madison, Wisconsin, did an eight-month stint in the small city, and found it to be the Capital of the American Runaways.

In Madison, they have a State Street, like any other major city, and it's the hangout spot. Teens from throughout America flock to this Midwest strip as if it's a pit stop along their adventure. Maybe it's due to the pot rally they hold around the capital each summer—who knows.

The teens are everywhere, despite the college crowd that the city revolves around. That's probably why the police don't mess with them that much, because these teens blend in with the young college crowd; white, black, and Hispanic runaways all in search of something, but what?

I met Justin, a fifteen-year-old white teen from Wyoming. Justin's parents had separated, and both had started dating other people even though they continued to live together. This was too much for Justin, especially when he found out his mother had become pregnant! He said he picked Madison because the fourth ride he got (hitchhiking) was going to Milwaukee and stopping in Madison to pick up someone, so he'd chosen his destination.

I met him that night and talked him out of killing himself. Justin was in James Madison Park with a loaded 38 special he'd stolen from his father. The gun was in his right hand, the trigger was cocked, and he was playing Russian roulette! After I slapped him off the bench he was sitting on, I grabbed the gun, and we talked until the sun came up. I took Justin to a friend's house, we called his family, and Justin's father wired me the money to get Justin on a Greyhound bus headed home. I never saw Justin again.

Two days after Justin left, I met Reggie. Reggie was a sixteen-year-old black teen who was a Crip gangster from South Central. He was on the run from his own gang, which thought he had shot at one of their own. He had family in Madison, who had promised him a place to stay when he called; however, this was because they didn't think he'd actually come. When he got there, they didn't want anything to do with him, thus he was homeless—so he said. (I never knew whether to fully believe their causes for leaving, but for whatever reason, they **did** leave and were homeless runaways.)

I met Reggie wandering around State Street the day after he'd arrived, and I took him to the Memorial Union.

The Memorial Union is a busy building on the college campus, basically for recreation, networking, and relaxing. Travel busses depart from there, there's a food and drink area, a video games section, an ice-cream counter, a banquet area, a lounge and patio area, a dance hall, and a free phone section. I slipped Reggie in there, found him an unused classroom upstairs, and kept him here for a while—almost two months! Really.

Within a week I got Reggie a job. With the help of a friend of mine (using his address), we got him a Wisconsin ID. And to this day, Reggie still lives in Madison with his new wife and two children. I see Reggie when I visit Madison and smile when we walk by the Memorial Union.

During that same month I met Constance and Maggie, both fourteen, Cuban cousins from Miami. Maggie was pregnant and Constance snorted heroin. At that time, Madison didn't sell heroin cheap, so Constance was going through withdrawal and insisted that they press on to Chicago. I got in touch with a friend in Summerset (a South Side poor housing project) who gave them both room and board until their family was able to come and get them. During the two-week stay, waiting on their family, Constance went through hell, but cleaned out her system. I made her sit for half an hour in a hot shower each night, which opened her pores and sweated out her habit. By the end of her first week, her appetite came back and she cried with happiness. Maggie was three months pregnant and wanted an abortion. I took them both on daily walks, until we came back one day and Maggie's parents were there. Maggie's father took their belongings and threw them into the car, and then turned around and snatched Maggie by the arm. He was about to hit her, until our eyes met, and he pushed her into the car. I hugged Constance and told her to stay away from heroin, but as the car screeched off, I saw the two girls' faces and knew they felt trapped. I never saw them again.

I then met Johnny, a sixteen-year-old break-dancer from Philadelphia. Johnny was mixed, tall, and an excellent graffiti artist, with one problem—he was on the run from the police!

Johnny's father had put him out because he'd done a huge mural on the outside of their community church. Though he'd been given consent by the church and paid, his father was disgusted. Johnny's father was an extreme religious fanatic who refused to accept Johnny the way he was. This severed their relationship for many years and crippled Johnny's artistic endeavors until he snapped, spray-painted his father's car, and broke all the windows. When the police came, instead of talking to them and explaining that his father had put him out at sixteen (which probably would have gotten his father a verbal slap on the wrist), he punched not one, but both of the officers and ran.

My first encounter with Johnny was on the rooftop of a Laundromat. This was my getaway spot (I had taken two fold-up chairs up there) to watch the scene. It was right next to State Street, which was busy, and I had a great view of the moonlit night. As I sat there trying to clear my mind, I heard someone climbing up my secret, homemade ladder (which I made out of wooden pallets). It caught me off guard, and my first impression was that it was the police! But it was Johnny, with two bags full of spray paint. He did a graffiti piece that had the Laundromat's name on it. We talked all night, and I realized the pressure his father had put on him. Johnny was crying out for help, but I didn't know where to start.

The next day when I went to my spot, there was a note tucked in between the plastic strips of my chair. It was from Johnny. The note thanked me for a sincere night of listening and said that he was on his way to L.A. to advance his artistic education. I never saw Johnny again.

There were so many other incidents with the homeless teens I encountered during my eight-month stay that I now truly feel this was why I left Madison. The pressure of helping so many; I couldn't keep up, nor did I want to, I simply wanted to be a teen myself. I suppose I ran from the responsibility of making their problems my problems.

When I got back to Chicago and Cabrini Green, I closed the door of my room and thought. There was so much pressure on me that it wasn't fair. Nobody, other than the runaways (and two good friends), knew what I had been through. I had been sent to Madison at sixteen to get away from the outrageous, wild, hardcore ways that had troubled my life at that point: gangbanging, selling drugs, stealing cars, getting locked up, getting suspended, busting parking meters, and causing shootouts. Instead of getting to Madison and clearing my mind, I only found other people's problems and made them my own. But something happened.

In those eight months I lived in Madison, Wisconsin, I started seeing others as real people with real problems, instead of just people being problems. I started understanding the concept of others in the world. But I had to leave a whole environment to grasp this. Sixteen is supposed to be a time when college decisions are being made, your first legal job, prom, and the things others feel should be important in your life. And though this may put stability in your life, there are too many that aren't living this way; too many. And these are the people I met, in the outside world, those I could not relate to at first because they were not from my immediate ghetto or life, or my perception of ghetto life! But then they became real people, and I couldn't let go.

I notice that a lot of runaways (and I met so many, literally hundreds) were running from family problems such as physical abuse, divorce, and alcoholism. The Hispanic teens were simply running from poverty and wanted to explore and work, though many were illegal. The black teens' parents were on drugs, so they had no parents, and they traveled with drugs so they could make money along the way. Story after story. I met teens from just about all fifty states, I kid you not. I even ran into a real-life *Coming to America* situation where I met a Moroccan prince whose father was a king. His plight was to leave his country and make it on his own; leaving everything to start with nothing and gain everything. In each of these cases, these teens were lonely and in search of attention. Meeting people offered new attention. Each encounter was a possible home or a possible death. The adrenaline ran high, but so did the search for belonging. So many teens stopped in Madison that I couldn't keep up.

I think what Madison offered was that it was friendly, you could be yourself, as opposed to L.A. or New York, where working on the strip was where many teens wound up. In Madison, since it was a smaller town, people were interested in meeting you, often opening their homes to you. In traveling, the younger generation had felt a sense of inspiration not offered by their families or surroundings. It was the norm to jump on a Greyhound and check out a new town or city. It was the norm to walk along the highway with your thumb out! To travel and meet people, like in the '60s, had experienced a resurgence, but in a new sense. People weren't naive, following an invisible peace campaign and hoping to score and network along the way. People were running from their problems in the hope of a better situation. And most of the people I met, I never saw again.

(Taking Action)

When I was ten, my mother and her boyfriend took me and my friend James to Circle Pines. This was a camping resort in Wisconsin. We rode up there in a Toyota pickup, with a top on the back of the truck, thus giving James and I our own space. We had everything back there: sleeping bags, camping gear, food, cards, radio, and walkie-talkies. This was our haven, and we rode in the back of the pickup to and from the resort.

There's a feeling that all of us have when leaving our neighborhoods and communities; hitting the highway for a getaway does something to us mentally. We feel as if we're leaving behind a stationary issue, something we'll have to deal with later; but for now we're free, in hopes of a new experience. The veil of old seems to have temporarily lifted the farther we go, and go...

Coming back from Circle Pines, James and I felt as if we were going back home to problems, thus we were sad and quiet. Finally, knowing that we were going to be needing gas soon, I told him that I had a plan. "Hand me a pen," I said, as we pulled into the gas station. We went into action.

Leaving the gas station, we felt a little better and waited for results. Fifteen minutes later, while driving down a peaceful major road, we heard tires screeching as seven police cars came from a side road, blasted their sirens, and chased us. At first, my mother's boyfriend didn't think it possible that they were after him. It was literally a scene from *The Dukes of Hazard*, as more cars skidded onto the road joining the chase. So he kept driving, which made it worse! Now twelve cars strong with their sirens blasting, they were right behind us.

"This is the County Police! Pull the car over, now!"

Though there was a thin partition and a sliding window between the back of the truck, where we were, and the front of the truck, where they were (and the sliding widow was closed), I still managed to hear my mother. "What? What's going on? What the hell is this?" she hollered, as her boyfriend pulled over.

"Slowly get out of the car, with your hands up!" the police yelled, with their guns drawn. "Now put both hands on the side of the truck, slowly. Keep them where we can see them!" Three officers ran to him, slapped handcuffs on him, and threw him on the front of one car.

They were about to put him in the back of the car when suddenly James flung open the back of the pickup and yelled, "Wait! We were just playing, we didn't mean it!"

My mother was snapping at this point and demanded to know what was going on. Three more officers came to my mother and explained that she would have to sit in the car until they could verify who her boyfriend was. They didn't put him in the back of the car, and they did take the handcuffs off as they ran his driver's license to make sure he was legit. We waited there for a half an hour before they finally let us go.

This is what had happened. When I asked James for a pen, I wrote the gas station attendant a note. It read: "We can't talk to you as we come into this store or they'll kill us! We've been kidnapped from our parents because we're rich. Please help us or you won't see us again...nobody will. Save us!"

As the attendant's eyes bulged, reading our note (grammatical errors and all), we pointed to our truck and left the gas station.

For James and me to get to this point, we must have been desperate. Desperate to hold on to peace of mind, happiness, simply to be away from the disappointments at home. At ten years old (with what I felt to be a stable home, compared to others), I dreaded going back to Chicago. The pressures I had seemed major at the time; so I can imagine how someone else in worse circumstances might feel. **Running** for a young teen means taking action, or taking matters into your own hands. This is what James and I felt we were doing at ten years old—taking action.

(Analysis)

So why are our teens running, and what does running mean? When the cycle starts young in running, it's hard to stop. The problem is that we can't say that these young teens are wrong for running. Many of us adults would run if given the opportunity. In fact, there's nothing wrong with running. Let me explain. At that point in a young person's life, running is not the same running that you and I perceive, because they're running for so much that they're not getting at home; thus, the search is on. So **running** translated to a young teen may simply mean exploring, seeking a new beginning, a new hope when their surroundings seem dark. Much of the time, the teens feel out of place or unwanted; other times, there's nothing at home to hold on to. Nobody's ever home, or so many people are doing their own thing that there's no time for family unity. As we can see, there are many reasons, and each of these is enough to push the teen from the residence. So if there's hope in hitting the highway, it had to have been brewing for a minute. Nobody runs to a different state they've never been to because of a new (sudden) dilemma in their household. Black urban teens—as I said before—have the loss or lack of parents due to drugs or poverty. Hispanics are fighting the same thing, as well as an inner battle of already feeling at the bottom of the totem pole, neither in a black world or a white world, and with the seclusion of speaking another language with only your family and friends—not the outer world. Hispanic urban teens often join gangs, and this becomes a way of life. White urban teens are running from pressure, from their parents or of an unstable environment, which can cause symptoms of the black and Hispanic plight: gangbanging, drugs, and homelessness. So it had to have been the buildup of these problems. But still, why running? Why not stay and try to change something?

Since we've already deciphered **running** as **exploring, seeking,** or **taking action,** how can we expect these teens to stay in what we feel to be chaos and they're at a breaking point, when they could easily seek new surroundings? These teens are smart enough to get away when it gets unbearable. So why do we get upset with them? We tell women in abusive relationships to do this all the time. "Just leave him, honey! Enough is enough, girlfriend! You have to finally stand up for yourself and get out!" And if they don't leave, we get mad, disappointed in them and angry at their weakness.

One thing that all these teens share before they hit the road is anger. One thing that we've done as a nation is to lower the age level of everything! We've lowered the age for marriage, we've lowered the age for divorce, we've lowered the age for giving responsibility, only because it's lowered on its own. Babies having babies, babies using drugs, babies being left at an early age, and babies simply not being able to be babies. So why shouldn't they be angry? We've taken a whole generation and said, "Grow up quick, and deal with it!" We've done this subconsciously, and then have the nerve to be disappointed in our children when things don't go as planned. For those that are running, I hope you find what you are looking for, and I'm sorry that you have to run...I am so sorry.

LOVE

L ove (luv) n 1. Warm liking or affection for a person, affectionate devotion.

The different forms of love are endless. Whether it's for a person, place, or thing, love affects how we view ourselves, society, and life.

Portraits of love are often deeper than we can imagine. Sometimes we have to put ourselves in another person's shoes to actually get just a piece of the understanding we may need.

Since I'm first focusing on two main aspects of love (from the white point of view to the ghetto point of view), we have to decipher how each one is instilled ethically, morally, and instinctively.

As whites grow up, since families are more stable, all extra energy has been channeled into love and support for the family. So actions are different pertaining to love. Without having to use the tough policies of the streets, whites are able to express (openly) their feelings toward one another. This is a beautiful thing, but it's still, in all, one form of love.

Because of a lack of luxuries, trust, commitment, responsibility, and direction, the ghetto can't possibly view love in the same way. First of all, let's try and analyze love for what it truly is. Love is perceived and conceived in the human mind; an emotion based on your experiences, surroundings, views, and morals. If your surroundings are hostile, wild, and uncontrollable (because of others' actions that alter your immediate lifestyle), then your mind has to do a certain amount of blocking out. You also don't allow yourself to feel vulnerable, which means there's a constant mental shield toward people in your community. So your sense of love is quite sheltered, and actually a different concept of love compared to whites. Those who live in the ghetto feel that it's a form of being "soft" to express emotions, when you have those that try to take advantage of you, taking your kindness for weakness.

Many times, the sense or form of love in the ghetto is expressed by loyalty, commitment, or respect. For men to pour out a little liquor **out of love** for a dead friend is a perfect example. Though it's in remembrance, it's the feeling of love that you had for this individual that connects you; the loyalty and respect. Out of love, you want your children to grow up quickly, to be hard and look out for those they shouldn't trust, because it prepares them for their surroundings. And most of all, out of love, you want your children to stay in school to get an education, so that one day they can make it "up" out of the ghetto. Though you love your mother or your children, it's more a feeling of security or strength, dependency and stability. That's why it becomes more hideous when your parents are on drugs, because this would have been the last resort of comfort. Now comes the boyfriend or girlfriend. Young teenage girls in the ghetto get caught in the love trap (as a security-dependency thing) with their boyfriends because this becomes not only an invisible father figure, but a hope of feeling love. Just a small piece will do, even if things aren't right between them. Thus these girls get pregnant, and the cycle continues.

To live in a white society does not necessarily mean being white. It basically means having a reasonable job (income), which in turn makes you middle class and allows you to live in a drug-free, gang-free community. With this comes the element of peace. Of course, it's fair to realize that because of this, everyday troubles don't cease; but you have to understand the domino effect that surroundings (and the lack of morals and money) have on young blacks. Kids are going to school with guns because they have to go through opposing gang territory to get there. So how can love actually be viewed the same, when lifestyles and emotions are not the same?

Picture being in the army, out on the field of combat, with bombs blowing up around you. People are dying, going AWOL, disappearing, and killing. Chaos surrounds you. Then suddenly, your partner gets shot, right beside you, instantly dying. You quickly feel remorse, as a thousand things run through your brain, because you loved the feeling of his immediate security, and your devotion to each other through this crazy mess was solid. Now it's gone, and as quick as you grieved, you have to immediately press on to ensue your own safety, not just physically but mentally. This is equal to the love that's offered in the ghetto. So many unpredictable things happen, so fast, because there's no longevity or stability to grasp onto—nothing concrete. Whites have to realize that this is neither a good thing nor a bad thing, simply a factual thing.

Pros and cons that offer balance come with both sides. For instance, with whites, having the emotional love thing so strong, people feel cheated when it's not offered constantly, or at least what they are used to. This leads to nervous breakdowns, seeking professional help, or sometimes, tragically, suicide. You hardly ever hear about blacks having nervous breakdowns, seeking counseling, or committing suicide. Not having the added benefit of unconditional love creates lower self-esteem, which reflects how you view others. If you're not receiving love, how can you offer love? And when and if you do, how can you be certain that it's the appropriate love that is necessary to keep a girlfriend, a spouse, or a child happy and satisfied? You can't. Also, because of the lack of love in the ghetto, blacks have built an "I don't give a fuck" attitude toward anything that may hurt their feelings, to keep them mentally safe. This closes off their love devices even more. Realize that it's survival in such a different environment, though!

There's another type of love that we in the ghetto have that one would consider ironic, and that is love for the ghetto itself.

Everyone in Cabrini Green (and all other projects) can relate to what I'm about to say. We have an invisible, underlining love for our community, despite its mishaps, tragedies and uncertainties. However, when we leave the projects, it's as if an invisible veil has been lifted, an open feeling of being able to take a clean breath. As we go back into the projects from wherever we went, it's the sad feeling of going back inside a dark place where we'd rather not be; a dilemma. All of us hate the aura of the projects, though we have a certain love for it. That's the ironic part.

Americans are an intricate bunch, and living with so many different lifestyles brings different levels of love, and what it means to each individual. Love in America is always classified as a sweet, deep, sensuous, open, fulfilling, warm, heartfelt, and unconditional emotion. But we must remember that love is a stage that you reach, which is hard to maintain over a long period of time, battling other emotions that you encounter daily. Those who learn to work with this emotion, balancing it with these others (over a long period of time) are to be commended, because these are the warriors that we as Americans need to embrace. Remember that love is a powerful emotion, because with it comes determination and perseverance, and through love the possibilities are endless!

(UNCONDITIONAL LOVE)

I know a black couple from the Midwest who for years had been trying to have a child. Finally, through tests, they realized that they couldn't for whatever reason, which started their adventure in adoption.

At first they were quite strict in defining what they wanted: a boy, and it had to be a black boy. But two years and five ethnic groups later, they had found everything but what they initially wanted. Finally, at the beginning of their third year, they received a call from the agency—an African American boy who was four weeks old and healthy, but had one problem. He was blind. The couple immediately broke down sobbing as they politely declined. Then there were two crack babies that were also black, but premature and needed too much medical attention; another decline. They thought that black babies were abundant! They were supposed to be. (There were three more, but they were much older than the couple expected or wanted; they too were declined.) Months went by as their relationship grew strained and silent.

Their lives seemed dark until one day the doorbell rang. The lady from the adoption agency came in holding a small bundle. The couple lit up as they looked at each other, tears of joy welled in their eyes. But as they went to the baby to view him, they were stunned. Uncovering his tender face, they saw "a vision in white" the man later told me, explaining his story.

The lady from the agency, still holding the child, explained that she had come from another soon-to-be adoptive family's house. No one was there (in fact, they'd moved without telling the agency), and she had called three days prior to confirm! Now they were gone. The house was only a couple of miles away, so she decided to stop by—something was telling her to.

As the three of them stood there, the black woman made the first move, reaching for the baby. "He had the prettiest light brown eyes I'd ever seen," she later stated. As she held the baby, the black man immediately came to her side, admiring the boy. For the first time in months they seemed pleased, as a unit, together. "Something went through my body," said the man. "We suddenly seemed to be a family." The baby was white, but as mature adults, they realized the huge obstacles ahead, and were ready to offer an unconditional love. They told the lady from the agency they'd let her know in the morning.

That night, though, there were so many questions and answers to be talked about. They were ecstatic; what possibilities, what challenge, what love they had to offer! They were filled with ideas and statements about schooling, birthdays, sleepovers, backyard cookouts, fishing, and so on, until they literally sat down to catch their breath. Suddenly, they looked at each other, knowing what the other was thinking. It wasn't that people might react funny, or even the rest of the family that might feel it awkward, but how the boy himself might actually feel when he was of age. The couple sat there and began to sob again. They wept until they were tired and fell asleep.

The man said he had a dream of holding his white child with joy, almost feeling as if he were just albino, proud to be his father. He awoke with tears of joy instead of pain. He gently woke his wife, his mind made up—they would go get their son and be a family.

The boy was eighteen days old when he entered their home, and Mathew (that's what they named him) brought joy to their lives.

I recently interviewed Mathew, now twenty-one, and my main focus was on some specific points in his life: first, when he found out he was adopted; second, when he realized the tremendous pressure that must have been on his parents; and third, his general life from the ages of ten to twenty.

Mathew: My life to me was no different than any other child's. I think there was so much love that my parents had to offer, I was just a happy child. And by the time I was seven, my parents noticed my many questions so we all sat down and talked. I learned what adopted was and why our appearances were different. I remember asking "Mom, I'm not going to have to go back, am I?" And with tears in her eyes, she smiled, hugged me, and said no.

I skipped a grade in school and entered high school at thirteen. This is when I used to see my parents actually go out of their way to be a part of my education. Sometimes I would sit back and ask myself, why are they trying to be so involved? Many times I enjoyed it, because they were hip and everyone liked them so much. But to me, it seemed they were overdoing it, and it hurt me to see them so tired. They were always involved in something...always. In high school, I realized how much pressure was hitting them. Pressure not to be just good parents, but to be better parents than the average! And for that I love them so much. I also started realizing the uniqueness of my adopted situation. As a matter of fact, I noticed that there were no other black families with white children. I had never heard about even one incidence.

I definitely wasn't a model student, but I tried to be. I also hung with the wrong crowd a few times and had to break away from that. I was an average teenager surrounded by peer pressure and the rest of the madness, but one thing my parents didn't do, and that was divorce, and I'd like to think I'm a part of that. I've had healthy relationships with women of all races, shapes, and sizes, and I'm here to tell you that each woman has her own unique qualities that make her special…regardless of race. Right now I'm in school, pursuing my law degree, and hope to be a great lawyer soon. (He smiled.)

As I looked at him and admired him, I wanted to embrace him, so I did. Mathew is a confident young adult who could have folded under his own pressure. Why are things like this? Why are my parents different? Why me? Why this, why that—and then simply to try and get away from the situation. But he didn't. Mathew grew up not only with the chaos in life we all endure, but with the remarkable difference of parents that is on the flipside of what our society expects as normal!

Just imagine this! I have never heard of a black couple legally (through paperwork) adopting a white child. I've encountered a couple passing away, and the godparents (who happened to be black) stepping in and taking on the responsibility; or even foster parents (host sites) who have licenses to watch kids for a brief period of time, possibly even a couple years—until they can be placed. But for a black couple to take a huge step in adoption, willingly, knowing from the start that they were to raise a white child (understanding society), realizing the large responsibilities of race relations, peer pressure, others' ignorance, and the painstaking dedication that would be involved is simply and thoroughly unconditional love!

We hear sometimes of negative feedback from the few black organizations concerning white parents adopting black children, and this too is wrong, for them to feel this way. Because I have many black friends who are quite pro-black, instilled in them by their white parents, yet they have a great deal of respect about it—the issue of culture is what we make it. All my black friends who have white parents say they actually deal with society much better because they have a somewhat bilingual handle on how to deal with people. Don't we all need this?

I agree that it's important to embrace your culture (to at least learn about it, and understand it), whether you are Hispanic, Irish, Italian, Creole, Korean, Jamaican, African American, etc. But it's equally important to realize that your culture is one of many. It's your responsibility to respect all cultures; this is what makes you a better individual. I've often asked these adopted kids if they'd ever want to meet their biological parents, and Mathew's statement basically sums up everyone's answer: "Right now, no, but possibly one day, to maybe know them on a friendship level. The parents I had offered me the love I needed and I couldn't have asked for anything more...I thank God for them."

Each of them mentioned their adoptive parents and the love they offered. The reply of an adopted generation (regardless of race) speaks for itself. These attacking organizations that are against race mixing have to realize this: In order for a couple to consider adoption, they have mostly gone through hell. They have suffered emotionally from mental and physical defeat, yet have remained strong; and still have to keep patience with the adoption agency. The only thing that could have kept a couple like this together is a strong unconditional love. Think about it; the things they went through merely to get to the adoption stage would have broken up just about any relationship, not to mention a marriage. The constant trying, though the sex is important—it's the results they're seeking, and not getting. The uncertainty if something is wrong with one of them—and then which one! The tests, the feeling of not being complete without a family, the failures, the emptiness and high hopes—and then the final analysis, willingly admitting and accepting defeat. What simple relationship could withstand this? By that time, they've come to the realization that if God or fate finally brings a child their way, they are going to be more than loving, more than gracious, more than humbled, more than encouraging, proud, dedicated, understanding, and strong. This is what being a parent is all about. I hope these organizations that are so stuck on race realize that the first stage of culture begins with love. These parents love their children unconditionally and feel it's their duty to offer every aspect of life, culture being one of them.

SEX AND RELATIONSHIPS

Many people have asked me to sugarcoat this chapter, but I won't. In fact, this chapter has to be pure, and raw! It deserves that much, because to be truthful, sex and relationships are affecting America as much as racism, if not more so. How we deal with sex and relationships is so diverse within our own cultures, that on an overall American view it's hard to grasp the concept; thus my job has been called!

(Sex and what it means)

Okay, my goal is to break down sex, as complicated a concept as it may be, and show the differences, meanings, and motives. Let's start first in the ghetto's age range of thirteen to twenty.

In the ghetto, it's as simple as this—sex is exercise. Before a young girl gets pregnant—whether at seventeen, eighteen, nineteen, or even fifteen—it's all about sex. Sex is looked at as the only positive thing to hold on to in the ghetto. If all else fails during your day—no money, arguing with peers and parents, the constant feeling of depression—that moment of sex, that single element within itself, is the only thing that is valid or makes sense. Thus, it's rampant. And after teenage girls find out that they can get paid for using their young bodies, they have sex for things they want and need: new fit, money, weed, jewelry, even the new Jordan's that are about to come out! Then comes the baby, the father runs from responsibility, and they both exercise with new partners. Sex in the ghetto is mandatory; it's drugs before the real drugs.

By fifteen, ghetto girls are experienced, trading stories of buck-wild sexual encounters. And since the age has dropped (as far as it being socially acceptable that kids are doing this; as we know, it's been happing all along), it's normal to have at least two children by the age of twenty. Thus, the comparison to drugs seems accurate, because sex is as necessary to young teens as drugs are to hypes. It is. If ghetto females don't get enough sex at fifteen and sixteen, they—like white women between the ages of twenty-five and thirty-five—get agitated, cranky, and miserable, because their bodies are used to getting it. The dependence on release, pleasure, and quick satisfaction is routine. And often, money and material things won't matter—that's why they have at least one partner they call their boyfriend, who doesn't have to pay for sex. With young females actually getting the notion through their heads that sex is worth money, it has run widespread throughout America's ghettos and has eliminated the '60s and '70s pimpology, and replaced it with self-pimpism. Eighty-five percent of the actual prostitutes that walk the strip don't use pimps, because these girls come from the ghetto and realize the independent significance and importance of self-prostitution.

For male ghetto youth, selling drugs is a means of survival, and it is accepted as being the norm in the hood. The money they accumulate is spent buying sex as much as it is buying clothes. These male teens have one main girlfriend whom they may not have to pay, but the rest will cost them. There will be times when you may not actually put money in the female's pocket, but you're still paying for the experience, by taking her to the motel and buying her what she smokes, drinks, or eats. This has already been calculated from your drug money as what you have to spend on weekly sex. It's mandatory. This is called **tricking off**.

Ghetto youth thinking of oral sex as acceptable has picked up over the last fourteen years. Previously, younger teens felt it was taboo and nasty, which kept it unexplored. But through music (especially female artists promoting it), money, word of mouth, competition, videos, movies, and simply growing up faster, it's now a type of sex that is desired. The number of ghetto youth experiencing oral sex is rising drastically.

Relationships do not become serious until the age of nineteen or twenty because of this constant sex. Although you may have a girlfriend, children, or a three-year relationship, it carries little weight. Generally, ghetto youth are not as quick to accept responsibility as white kids are. And when they finally do (even the slightest bit), they immediately want to settle down. They often get married and end up feeling over the hill by twenty-two, which in some ways they are (theoretically and physically)! This is how ghetto teens grow up faster than white teens—by force.

Early-age sex in the ghetto is as much the ghetto as the ghetto itself.

White teens from thirteen to twenty are less sexually active simply because their time is spent on more productive and constructive activities. Lately, we hear more and more about white female teens getting pregnant, and statistics have certainly shown a drastic increase, but still and all, they are far lower than the normal—and ever-rising—statistics of the ghetto baby boom!

On the reverse side, white teens have always been more passionate in their relationships, offering more affection—physically and emotionally—which in turn has led to oral sex. So yes, white youth have been active in this arena much longer. They are somewhat less likely to have intercourse than ghetto youth. If you're not so dependent upon money, your life isn't overwhelmed by depression or fear, and you don't already have kids, then you're just not in the same boat as ghetto youth—and don't (can't) view sex the same way. How could you? Your life is structured and so is that of your mate, so free time means just that—free time—which is the time when you and your mate can get away, meet up, and do whatever. Don't forget, there's more family stability and the parents are quite involved, and the thought of a female being pregnant while still in school causes panic in the world of white teens and parents!

Due to the structure of white society, white youth are more likely to have had classes and lectures pertaining to AIDS and STDs, and their parents are more open to talk about these. There also seems to be an element of fear instilled in white youth with regard to the whole concept of sex, possibly on purpose.

White youth are having sex, but do not have the same level of dependency or frame of mind as ghetto youth. Yet.

As we look upon ghetto adults, those who have made it that far without ending up dead, in jail, or moving out of the ghetto, we're left with hardened hearts. These adults have children—usually two sets of children by different people—have been married and are still not divorced, have low-paying jobs (if that), often have criminal records, and are possibly on welfare. They simply want a partner to call their own, someone to struggle with. What's interesting now (because we are in a transitional stage) is watching ghetto teenagers become adults—over twenty-five—because unlike their parents who get high, they don't. So we now have two sets of ghetto adults to look at: those from twenty-five to thirty-five, and those thirty-five and older.

Ghetto women who are thirty-five and older (and not addicted to drugs) do two things:

1. They look for an older man—someone financially stable, more mature, and willing to accept responsibility for her and the children. Sometimes it may simply be an agreement that he pays her for sex, and that's the basis of their relationship.

2. They go the other route—wanting and needing to feel young, they will date only younger men. Because people their age and older get high, they feel like outcasts and crave being around people who have similar interests. These women enjoy the company, sex, and excitement of a younger mate, and are looked upon and referred to as vets. They will pay for what they want and have no problem sporting their mates.

Since these ghetto adults thirty-five and older have been true soldiers of their past (and have grown out of their past ways), their children haven't been invisible and are now teenagers; whereas whites at this age are usually just having children. So, dating is tricky for these ghetto women because there's a lack of black men, and those men who have made it out of the ghetto, with no children (seeming to be the perfect mate), aren't usually interested in the ghetto females who come with baggage. Those who keep their options in the hood rely on lovers they call "friends" (simply a booty call). It limits relationships.

Now, with the twenty-five to thirty-five ghetto adult, it's all about going out and partying. Your "smack in the face" transition stage (nineteen through twenty-four) is over. So you had your few years of settling down and are either married, divorced, cheating, or creeping, and you are again ready to take on the world. Thus, you end up making or having more kids and getting into different relationships. And though you feel wiser, you actually repeat your transition stage all over again.

In the ghetto, a wave of change that alters through the years is the age difference—young women (including teens) going out with older men, sometimes much older. One might think that it has always happened, and there may be instances when it has. The majority of young ghetto women mature mentally by fad! What's in at the time is what determines the yea or nay. In all ghettos, there will be years when you can't pay a young female to talk to an older guy, but there will be waves when all the young girls have an older man. There are so many things in the world that domino effect this wave altercation that it's hard to tell when it's going to come, stay, stretch, or fade. You will simply have to pay attention.

(THE MYTH)

First of all, let me say the Myth about black men having bigger private parts simply isn't statistically or factually true on an overall basis. Sorry. Being in the ghetto for more than twenty years, having been to the penitentiary, endured strip searches, been in and out of the county jail, been to boot camp, and been subjected to shakedowns—it's something a straight man just notices, and anyone who has gone through these and says he hasn't noticed is lying like a vic and must be ashamed or something!

The bottom line is that men of each race have bigger parts than others. There may very well be instances when black males will be the subject of this, and sometimes it will be true, but it's because they've been momentarily targeted. Ask any black woman, and she will tell you that there have been many times when she's been disappointed with her so-called brothers.

How the Myth about black males—and their privates—ended up being blown out of proportion is because black males, until the Civil Rights Movement in the '60s, have received the worst end of the stick here in America, and to this day are still in a struggle. Because these whites (and when I say whites, I'm referring to a certain class—high society and up, possibly the powers that be) felt that they owed blacks at least a positive endeavor through the slightest public gesture, pornography being one of them. This was also done to harness the financial climb. It's been the scare of elder white America to envision a well-hung black male or Latino having sex with a white female. And this is what sold, because these are the ones whites felt threatened by! Thus this market was targeted; thus this process and era increased; thus it became commercial. What we've seen in videos, read and seen in porno magazines, and heard by word of mouth was spread like anything would here in America— by publicity—and whites cashed in. It's been overdone now, often to the point of being comical, even sarcastic, for white-collar magazines (sometimes black magazines not even realizing it) to make fun of the penis syndrome, as we can call it. Enough is enough, because when you're making fun of something, you need to realize there are actions, notions, and results behind it. If you're continuing to make money off something that you're not a part of, stop. Enough Myths, let's work with facts.

(PLAYERISM)

Since I said that I wouldn't sugarcoat shit in this chapter, I will continue to give it to you raw—so listen; it's about to get deeper.

Like anything else, "Playerism" has been exploited here in America. Playerism (the act of playing the field, with more than one lover) is at an all-time high, but more so in people's minds. They perceive themselves as a player, when in actuality it's irresponsibility.

Everyone in the hood wants to be a damn player! Since we're all hiding our feelings (or trying to), this is one of the best ways to cover up any indication that you care, or have feelings for someone. It's spawned another interesting concept, the "**HATER**." It's similar to the respect/disrespect parallel I mentioned earlier in the Respect chapter. Respect and disrespect have been tied together in the same way that Player and Hater have. Don't forget that the word Hater is used by the Player and is seemingly attached to the Player concept, because anything and everything becomes a Hater! Anything not going your way—anything at all that is against you—is a Hater! There were T-shirts: "Beware of the Player Hater," "Haters on the Rise," and "Definition of a Player Hater." Rap songs came out, talking about the Haters as much as the Players, interweaving the two until the ideology was as one. Superman and Lex Luthor, cop and robber, good guy and villain! The problem went deeper, since in actuality both could be viewed as good guy and bad guy, simultaneously, depending upon which side you were on!

A Hater is someone who supposedly doesn't like the fact that you're a player, and whom you often accuse of "hating on you." This basically means that they've busted you out, caught you in the act of cheating, exposed you, or tried to get you to do the right thing in the hope of changing you, pulling you up, or showing you a better way to go about it. The problem is, since everyone thinks they're such a player, the constructive criticism seems meaningless and instantly gets brushed to the side (negatively), and those doing the criticizing are denounced as being Haters.

Playerism is nothing new, but, as I've told you, the ghetto takes a concept and adds its own twist—too much damn twist! With the ghetto being a hard, cold, and lonely place, playerism was absorbed into its own interpretation—even creating something of a following—and became a new fad, with a new meaning! A phony one! Ghetto blacks have made this whole idea hip and damaged its actual intent. Being a Player has gone from being responsible—dealing with multiple relationships maturely and respectfully—to not giving a fuck about hoes! This not-giving-a-fuck attitude has created a scapegoat, with ghetto men distancing themselves further from responsibility. Since the overwhelming majority of ghetto men and women are now into this Playerism ideology (and many teens are growing up into it), with its damaging wall of isolation, mistrust, and disrespect, how can we expect there to be any positive ghetto relationships leading to marriage? We can't. So where has this left us?

With our ghetto youth being brought up into this ideology, we've been left with them not knowing the difference, and thinking that this is the way it's supposed to be. They'll never know the real virtue of being a positive player. That's fucked up. If no one is laying down the real "game" and groundwork for these brothers and sisters) to manifest, then it can only get worse. As it stands, there are many men who claim to be players, try to be players, and want to be players, but get caught up in the wrong emotions and go out the back door like straight-up wimps! These are the men who buckle under pressure and beat their women; who say they don't care, but as soon as their women leave, they try and force them back. These men end up with restraining orders and jail time—and in the end, they blame it on the Haters!

Playerism is supposed to be about handling emotions. Playerism is supposed to be about being fair. Playerism is about self and what you can offer others positively. Although sex is a part of Playerism, it's merely a side effect that magnifies it. Playerism is about life and balance, and about getting experience under your belt and learning from it. Playerism is about patience and dedication, about understanding yourself and others. And most of all, playerism is about pain—learning to let go, and being happy with your ex-partners' happiness. Many people are not cut out to be players, and this is fine. Respect this part of the game. Just realizing that you are not a player and accepting it makes you a player in your own way. You are one of the blessed ones who will be able to appreciate the depth and fulfillment of a monogamous relationship! Often, these are the real players.

Many of the men I've known while incarcerated in the county jail were locked up for petty crimes: traffic, panhandling, loitering, possessing less than four bags of weed, domestic, simple stealing (food), graffiti, participating in marches and protesting, scalping tickets, etc.

Some of these guys were lucky and got house arrest, but many couldn't (they had no home phones). So they sat. These men had girlfriends and wives, like anyone else, but the wrath of jail crushes the best of relationships. From the time a man is thrown in the back of the police car, his girlfriend is either going to leave him at that moment, or hold on as long as she can—thus she is incarcerated also. And for her, this mental incarceration is as depressing and damaging as his physical incarceration.

The first thing that happens (if you don't get house arrest and you do have a home phone) is you're on that phone like white on rice, because that's your main connection to the outer world! But what ends up happening is that you let yourself in for the big letdown—the phone block. (A real player handles responsibility and limitations, and knows when to ease up—on anything.)

You are allowed to call a number only a certain amount of times per week. When you get close to this limit, they'll give you a few warnings, and if you persist, the block immediately comes on. The block will not be removed until the phone bill is paid. This is when the inmate snaps and goes through a thang! Because now he's been further isolated from society, leaving mail and weekly visits as his only resort!

Mail becomes hope. You literally get hooked on mail as if it were drugs, and are deeply hurt when you're expecting some and none comes. As mail time nears, you start getting nervous, hoping they will call your name. When they finally come in, you hold on to each and every word, memorizing other people's last names (because it's usually the same crowd that gets mail). Sometimes, when the officer gets to the end and your name hasn't been called, you blame him, the people in the jail's mail room, even the mailman. You're traumatized.

The same thing with visits. Inmates get visits once a week and visiting day is a big deal—more hoping, anticipation, and nervousness. If your visitors don't come, you're crushed and your mind runs wild. Your girlfriend is cheating, she's no good, she never really cared, she's a hoe! You think the worst and you're deeply hurt, trying to find a reason, but there is none.

Depending on how long you're gone, many things change with your previous relationship. Many men with phones tell the tale of another guy picking up the phone, but not accepting the call (we can hear who says hello, then the jail collect-call service comes on). Soon after comes the Dear John letter, and before you know it, the woman's completely out of you life—a memory. This is when all the jailhouse tales of being a player are put to the test, because as soon as these girlfriends leave, you find out how emotionally attached these men were. Some break down like little bitches, others keep talking about how they don't give a fuck—over and over and over. But the real player will accept it. Although it may be hard for a moment, he will be happy that the woman found someone, because he knows that he will always be able to do his thing with her whenever he comes home. Period.

One of the worst dilemmas for inmates (which has damaged relationships and ended them faster than planned) is that they don't fully realize that the world doesn't stop because they're in jail. That no one has to come and visit them, that people don't owe them squat—even if they didn't do the crime they're accused of. The world isn't fair; they've got to remember this.

Saying goodbye to a loved one is hard, and being incarcerated makes it worse. Often, because of our being taken so abruptly, our girlfriends end up with someone similar to us: with possibly same complexion, hairstyle, look, dress code, and style. Our girlfriends are in search of someone to fill the void while we are away. Though we may have children with these women, years, precious memories, and more, it's unfair for them to hold on if they're miserable (especially if they've been holding on longer than a year). Just let go. But let go as friends; that way, there is respect on both sides.

Night after night you will have emotional dreams. These dreams will reveal your pain as you wake up teary-eyed. Dreams of home and family, dreams of your wife and making love to her, and sometimes dreams of losing her to someone else and being unable to remember what they looked like once you awaken. Though you've talked yourself into letting go of a loved one, your subconscious reveals your inner emotions that stab at your heart. Being a player deals with self and how you handle not just women, but life and your interactions within your surroundings.

I've read just about every penitentiary book ever written. Some are dark, some are depressing, some are over-exaggerated, and many are boring. Why? Because they don't deal with emotions., They deal with detail after detail, and on and on—never connecting the two; the encounter with the location, the attitude with the situation, and the impact with the predicament. Authors! Please remember, everything is interrelated, and incarceration that is detrimental to rehabilitation, to hope, to strength, and to self. Often people will get married in the penitentiary to keep themselves afloat- to survive. To live.

Being incarcerated is a time to reflect. It's a shame there aren't more programs in jail to counsel, to listen, to let people know that this isn't the end. To simply vent. This is a lonely time when men need help with their manhood, and this too is an indication of how they will be once released back into society.

(OVERVIEW)

The reason I didn't look at the white connection or point of view in "Playerism" is because I wanted to focus on the ghetto, where the ideology has been altered. And if you notice, "Jailhouse Relationships" also has been untouched by whiteness, only because in jail, all are equal! Being incarcerated is being incarcerated, no matter what race, creed, or color, and relationships are damaged.

America thrives on people and people thrive on relationships. America thrives on sex and sex thrives on relationships. Sex and relationships are together, yet they are also separated—often too separated. The future can only hold damaging results if this connected disconnection continues. We can only have sex as long as we don't go together; we can only go together if we have sex; and if we do have sex, we can break up and still have sex. So hell, let's forget the relationships and just all have sex! NOT.

Relationships offer support, and whether or not you believe in soul mates, it's the connection between two people that strengthens our spirits. Humans share interests, beliefs, emotions, and time in building a relationship. Relationships have strengthened couples in the ghetto and offered the support they've needed to move out; they have taken trailer park trash who have a goal to Wall Street; and they have encouraged those in marriage to adopt a needy child, with love! Relationships offer insight and help each person benefit from the other; hence, the phrase "my better half."

Let's get this shit together, because relationships transcend racism! All racists have relationships, and all races have racists. So, to those phony-ass racists, I say: Get on the ball with your own problems and stop getting into other people's problems. You're wasting our time, and believe me, we are the majority—those who want things to work for all of us! The majority!

We (of all races) have taken relationships for granted here in America, and have based everything on sex. Building a relationship is special because these are the people you can count on. Let's think again about our relationships in the twenty-first century, because as real people, with real emotions and real problems—it's what we need.

SIMILARITIES

Since I've pointed out some of the differences between races, it's only fair that I point out the similarities. Which, in a good sense, are endless! There are too many similarities to print, so let us look at the most important factual ones!

As human beings on this Earth, regardless of race, we all depend on many things, air, water, and food being the top three. Every human on this planet has type A, B, AB, or O blood, which can be used by all races as long as the type matches. We all have emotional responses to what is inflicted on us by others, which in turn produces what we inflict on others. Women of all races are the bearers of children. Regardless of slang, trailer-park lingo, Ebonics, or regional dialects, we as Americans understand and speak English as our number-one language. We all believe in marriage when we feel we've found the right person! We have our children get their shots so they won't get diseases. We all wear clothes because it is the socially acceptable custom. We feel embarrassment and loneliness. Each of us has emotions, no matter how bottled up or open—we have them.

We as a country pay attention to TV, newspapers, sports, comedy, and the weather. We follow styles and fashion, and many of us own cars. We all search for answers, whether large or small. We have faith in a divine creator, and though there are atheists that share scientific beliefs with other atheists, they're as in tune with society as much as the next person! We all sing to our favorite songs, cheer for our favorite teams, follow our favorite actors, drink our favorite drinks, eat our favorite foods, and laugh when something's funny! Each of us searches for forms of increasing our financial status, whether it's panhandling, working a minimum-wage job, corporate takeovers, or knocking off Pauly for advancement in the family! Whether you're trading elephant tusks in Africa, heroin in Nigeria, or stock market tips in London, our planet revolves around wealth and gain. All of us are affected.

Many of us, regardless of race, have brown eyes, dimples, glasses or contact lenses, gray hair, children, pets, hair loss, cancer, fat stomachs, buck teeth, dyslexia, crossed eyes, knock-knees, bad breath, asthma, memory loss, addictions, stress, headaches, back pain, handicaps, blindness, deafness, infertility, impotency, acne, arthritis, anorexia, dandruff, and warts. Many of us have the same needs, want the same sex, are the same height or weight, have the same cravings, names, talents, or interests, and have the willingness both to offer unconditional love and to be negative.

In actuality, we are more alike than we'd like to admit. So what is it that makes us different? Besides our visual effect (because we obviously notice the difference in skin tone), we have one thing that separates us: Our minds. It simply boils down to just that, our brains. The visual effect can only go so far. It's the mind that computes how we're supposed to feel toward an object. We must educate ourselves and understand that there are too many similarities between us to fall into the mental trap of "difference." Control your mind. Think of the similarities we all have when noticing the visual effect.

(THE BIGGEST SIMILARITY)

The biggest similarity we all have is the will to live and survive! There are three things that make up this concept:
1. Wanting achievement and acceptance in life.
2. Not being able to accept death as an option.
3. Our "spirit" or "lifeline" (as we call it) gives us a taste of life within, connecting us to the life outside. Our body craves this force and knows it cannot be functional without it.

The will to stay afloat has been called a few things: spirit, aura, lifeline, and vibe. Regardless, this life force invisibly connects you to the life around you because **it is of this**, and one day it will be set free, when the body that harnesses it dies. Your spirit is simply a chemistry of perfect energy; thus, it is of God, because it is of the universe and perfect. Anything perfect is positive, and anything positive is of great balance. This is where your brain comes in. Since your positive factor is your spirit, life has to offer immediate balance, which is your brain. Now, you can either make it work with you by supplying positive thoughts, which continue to give you great balance, or you can struggle against your positive spirit by being negative in thought, perceiving the worst out of life. Your brain can either aid your positive endeavors or ruin them, and you, in the process! I don't care who you are—Jeffrey Dahmer, Charles Manson, or Adolph Hitler—we all have spirits that are positive, and this is something you cannot change! What screws us up and make us negative are our mental concepts, which throw off our balance completely. Negative thoughts bring negative actions. However, you, as a human on this Earth, have a battle—not just with self, but to bring out the best in others as well. No matter how negative someone is, I realize that their spirit is positive, and sometimes can be influenced by my positive energy. Think about it. Have you ever been around someone so negative, so phony, or so evil that you just didn't want to deal with them, but when you did, you noticed a difference made in them by your positive energy? I don't care how negative they are, simply by being around a positive influence, something happens.

For example, when I was incarcerated in Cook County Jail recently, I went to segregation (which we call the "hole") for fighting. No, I didn't beat up Big Ray. I went for defending a friend, when this so-called "Black Bruce Lee," which is what he called himself, tried to take my friend's breakfast. (He won't be trying to take anyone else's breakfast.) I was sentence to ten days in the hole, but ended up doing fourteen because the computers were down. I ran into a guy who is notorious in Cabrini Green for being a stone-cold killer, which he is. This man has been doing MOB hits for his organization for years (Chicago street gang), and is proud of it. As I came through the door, he immediately spotted me through his chuck hole. "Ay! K-So! What up, fool?" he hollered. "Man, these bitches got me in here for fuckin' up one of the officers!"

They locked me in my empty, one-man cell and I listened to his story through my chuck hole. But he jumped from his story (about getting to the hole) to all the dirt he'd done in the hood. We hollered through the chuck holes for a couple of hours, and then I told him that I'd talk to him in the morning, it was late.

In the hole, you're locked in your cell twenty-three hours a day, and only allowed to come out for a single hour to shower. If you're lucky and the officer is cool, he'll unlock a lot of the cells so that you can talk to the other inmates before being locked in for another twenty-three hours. Otherwise, they only let out two at a time.

So while lying on my bunk after talking to this cold-blooded killer, I was wondering how his balance had allowed him to live for so long without being popped off like the rest of the brothers in the hood that had done major dirt. What goes around around. And since he hadn't been popped off yet, I vowed to see if I could change this killer's attitude. I realize a lot of people (especially those who know him) would be thinking, why are you trying to be a hero? Fuck him. Let that motherfucker die! But that's the thing about being positive, there's a need to give it to others. Some of the hardest tests are the ones you feel you can't face or win.

When our doors popped in the morning, I was slow getting out. In the two minutes it took me to grab my toiletries, I already heard his voice snappin' on another inmate. "Nigga, I'll knock your bitch ass out!" he wailed from across the dayroom, because someone had beaten him to the shower. He was then about to do what he said, until I intervened. I pulled him to the side and snapped on him about not making it any worse for himself, he was already in the hole! He immediately started talking about Cabrini Green and what we were missing. As he talked on and on and on about his shootings and his hits, I finally looked at him and said, "You're saying all of this as if you're proud. That's nothing to be proud of, man." It was as if my words went in his ears, permeated his brain, sank deep down inside, and numbed his speech. He looked at me and was about to continue, but was stuck. I, seeing that the shower was open, pointed and said, "Go ahead, grab it while it's open," and walked off. I did this repeatedly through my fourteen-day stay in the hole. It never ceased to amaze me, the look on his face each time I did this. You could tell that no one had ever talked to him like that, with positive comments that went against everything negative he'd just excitingly stated. At times, he seemed to want to reply with something positive, but caught himself. Everyone was scared of him, and why shouldn't they be? Dude was actually a real-life killer. And this was why it meant so much to me to hit him with some positive work—because he was from my hood and I was the only one he'd listen to. (Remember, too, that the tone and mannerisms I used with my positive comments were buck wild. Don't think for one minute that it was subtle talk. It wasn't. You can be hardcore while being positive; many times you'll have to be.)

By my seventh day he'd made some progress. Instead of war stories when he saw me, he'd talk about Cabrini and a lot of good times. Sometimes he'd drift, but I'd pull him back.

On the thirteenth night, he showed me some love (one of our Cabrini handshakes, with a sincere hug that I had never seen him give anyone, not even his mother) before we were locked up. When I lay down on my bunk, I looked up at the empty bunk on top of mine (we had steel bunk beds) and noticed—for the first time—that someone had burned in "God is good all the time." I couldn't help but agree. The next morning I left and went back to population.

Whether or not anything I said made a lasting impact, I won't know for a while—maybe never. But in my mind I know I tried, thus staying positive. Maybe he'll get killed when he gets out. Hopefully not, but at least one person from Cabrini came to him with some positive shit. It starts with rehabilitation, and rehabilitation comes from self, and self comes from spirit...

It's the biggest similarity we all have.

Similarities are what makes the world go around. Different countries monopolize and use forms of currency similar to ours; people speak to each other in different languages, communicating globally; children are born and raised, and families are enhanced; people work for a salary, love from the heart, cry from pain, long for attention, and smile with happiness. We are all so similar, yet our minds try to categorize our backgrounds and separate us.

Think about the similarities, because there are so many. Based on how you perceive, it's regenerated and thrown back into the world and into the minds of others. This is not an accident; this merely shows us that we are a part of something much bigger and we are all affected!

PROBLEMS

This book is aimed at solutions (as I've often mentioned), but, as we all know, solutions are derived from problems. So this chapter is aimed at the problems, even within ourselves, which in turn offer solutions. Some of these problems are dealt with and taken from certain chapters in the book, the rest are problems we need to deal with.

* I've lost a lot of good male friends. I've lost a lot of close female friends, along with my daughter and grandparents. While incarcerated I lost just about all of them, except the loss of my daughter, which happened while I was free.

The problem is that you're supposed to be innocent until proven guilty, but (as we all know) as soon as you're taken into custody, you're guilty until proven innocent! Due to this attitude, the treatment you receive is despicable. And if you have a loved one die while you're incarcerated, there's no outlet for this, yet it happens every day!

Then they say that the only funerals you are allowed to attend are those of immediate family, meaning parents, brothers and sisters, or kids—that's it! And half the time, they don't finish the paperwork soon enough, so you still miss out! When someone who is not immediate family dies—uncle, grandparent, girlfriend, stepchildren, best friend, aunt, or cousin—why aren't there special people in the jail that you can talk to and vent your frustration? They always want to try and send you to church, to some two-bit storefront preacher who talks to you for two minutes and then he's got to go to lunch, or a counselor who knows nothing about family counseling, only how to get you a free phone call.

My mother doesn't know this, but when her mother died while I was locked up, I almost went crazy. Although I was deeply hurt by the loss of my grandmother, I was more hurt by how it affected my mother. The same thing when my grandfather on my father's side recently passed away. To call home, yet not be able to attend the burial or mourn with the family, was traumatic for me (though I held it in, and no one but my cellmate knew).

The problem lies in the concept of being locked up (out of sight, out of mind) and society's perception of this ("They have no rights! They're obviously guilty or they wouldn't be locked up in the first place."). This perception brings forth resentment from the media, the public, and the powers that be—that inmates are not to be treated (or trusted) as people, we are outcasts of society, and this is acceptable…we have no rights.

So I urge city officials and politicians to look into this before deaths start occurring inside the jail from resentment.

* Which brings us to another problem that needs to be addressed: weakness. Children are made to go to Sunday school, pushed to learn the Bible, taught to confess their sins, etc. The responsibility of religious education becomes a distraction from growing up and being an adolescent, and thus becomes a weakness. When you're a teenager, having faith in God is often not "in." So as you get older (still not believing in God), you happen to get a good job, a wife, and kids, and continue to live your life. What becomes your motivation and drive? A promotion, your kids' college funds, or new home? Well, you end up getting the promotion, the kids are finally off to college, and you've been in your new home for five years. But something is missing. You've tried to stay busy all these years, working your butt off to block out what you felt was a weakness. The connection between faith and weakness has been ingrained in you for so long that it's not an option at this point. In fact, you feel that the weakness would be much worse if you were to even think about faith at this late stage.

* One problem that upsets me is that there's a difference in "expectations" between whites and blacks, and not just in the ghetto. Middle-class blacks on down the line are satisfied with mediocre jobs and positions in life. To be the assistant instead of the assisted; to be a manager at McDonald's for nine years without looking into buying the damn store; to get a GED and think that you've made it; to work at the car wash and talk about how dirty someone's car is and you don't own one; to have your son working as a bag boy at twenty-eight years old, and you go brag to everyone that he has a job. These are the things people actually do. The sad part is that, in their minds, it's acceptable to never advance. Due to their lowered expectations, they literally can't conceive of it.

She's fine being the assistant nurse; as long as she has a job and makes reasonable money, she can't picture being the head nurse. To be a manager at McDonald's is the bomb for some people; the title of manager, who could ask for more? Screw that. Look into owning the joint! I realize that a lot of people think a GED is all you need, but man, don't stop there, my brotha! I ain't even gonna talk about the car wash. And to you precious moms who are glad your baby got off his ass at twenty-eight and got a little job, bless you, but get on his ass to pay rent, the phone bill, and whatever else you can get out of him, because I know he's still living with you! Right!

The point is, in order for minorities to be equal, you have to look at the big picture for what it is, not what you feel comfortable with temporarily. Whites seem to set their goals at an earlier age, and the stability of their environment enables them to reach a certain level of comfort, so that they can focus their energy on maintaining their achievements. It's something of a reliable domino effect that's not offered in the ghetto.

However, knowing that, I want minorities to at least try and look at the big picture, and realize that it's not as far-fetched as you've mentally made it.

* Society has connected faith with the church, God, Jesus, responsibility, Sundays, dressing up, communion, singing, commandments, brotherly love, and all that they advocate. So if you have **big brother** already translating faith for you, it's adding to the misrepresentation of what it could mean to you.

* "But Mama, you said you was gonna watch her today!" cried Shante, the voice of the typical twenty-first century ghetto teen, at the perceived injustice of being denied what she feels to be her right—leaving her daughter with grandma—so that she can enjoy her usual free time!

As a nation (and not just minorities, but focusing more so on minorities), we've slowly lost a valuable family asset—good ole grandma! With times moving faster, teens getting pregnant at a younger age, and unstable morals, living conditions, and employment, good ole grandma today is not the same as what we had fifty years ago. Much has happened to alter this:

1. Let's first classify grandma. We're talking about the mother of the teenager with the baby; in actuality, the **baby's** grandmother.

2. Since now our teens are parents, the age of grandparents has dropped—to what used to be the norm for having a baby, thirty to forty years ago! This means that they're still dealing with their lives, and are not as stable as society's general concept of "grandma." And how could they be, at this early age?

3. So grandma has vanished, to be replaced with "grandma!" Which grandma? The baby's great-grandmother! Yes, the great-grandmother has to step in. And since times are harder, this too is unstable.

So a generation gap has reversibly flipped with American minority moms, but in doing this we've not allowed time to grow and learn. (Meaning, since the age has drastically dropped there's no in between time for maturity between the grandma and her daughter to set in; both are still experiencing life as young individuals.) We have to get used to this new era, at least for now, until times change and things can gradually get back in order.

* The problem is that middle-class or upper-class Americans can't see or won't admit that there's as big a problem as there actually is with the ghetto (lower-income communities, not just black), and enough is enough. This issue simply cannot be overlooked. It is crippling our nation. I realize that many whites have little interaction with minorities, because of where they grew up and where they live. So, in never dealing with another race or culture, I see how it could be perceived that all of life's trials and tribulations seem to be too much. How can I deal with another race when I can barely deal with myself, let alone my own race? If you've never dealt with blacks (or minorities), and all of a sudden issues arise about race relations, I can understand how it would repel you. However, you have to understand our plight, and the need to build race relations, defuse racial tension, and prosper as a nation—everyone. You'd be shocked at how the domino effect would positively affect your life. We're only asking that you keep an open mind and try to block out the inevitable. You will benefit. We will benefit. America will benefit. The ghettos across America need help

* This country was based on a dream (with liberty and justice for all), and if our forefathers talked the talk, but didn't walk the walk, it is up to us to make it a reality! If you let many of the negative things in this country affect you—turning your back and not giving a damn about our country (yes, your country, too; where you and your family live, and where you lay your damn head)—then you have added to the problem, and we're not going to pamper your sorry ass! Straight up.

Being an American has to mean something again, but on our terms and with our concepts, because we live here. Yes, it's a shame to not want to "represent" where you're from, because of the ugly injustices your country bestows. That's why it's time that we (the new generation) get mentally prepared to take back what's ours: financially, morally, spiritually, properly, and respectfully.

In doing this, one problem that needs to be tackled immediately (because it is affecting much of our economy, nobility, and structure) is illegal aliens. This should be one of our first issues to seriously address.

My heart goes out to those in search of financial gain, better living conditions, and the fulfillment of a dream, but as a nation we've put ourselves in a bind by letting our neighbors infiltrate. We can no longer do this.

I have many friends who are living in America illegally, and I don't know what I would do if I were to lose them. However, as an American, I know the importance of standing strongly within our own house before we can help others.

We're in a critical time, and it's our job to focus more on illegal aliens, immigrants, and those not registered to be here, the reason being that it simply allows our crooked business owners the chance to exploit them.

1. Many Americans are bumped from basic jobs by illegal aliens; and these illegal aliens are being paid less than American citizens.
2. Most are being paid under the table, which excludes the company's taxes so businesses are getting over.
3. They're having more children and increasing the population, yet don't count on our census.
4. Often when they're returned to their home country, they come right back.

These four are the basic but definitely serious issues.

Being a humanitarian puts me in a tough position with the illegal aliens I know (not to mention my own personal endeavors) regarding this major problem; because it is.

Our world cannot change overnight, but many of our concepts can. If there are things we do that may seem stern, overrated, structured, or prudent, that's because we (Americans) are in a transition of powerful change—regulating a new, "**us.**" Later we can open old doors, but now it's time for spring cleaning.

* I know I mention Upski a lot, but I'm truly upset with a project he had a few years back.

Upski was supposed to show white America that the supposedly hardcore ghettos weren't that bad. He was to hitchhike around America and go to these hoods to prove his point—simply by walking through them! He hit nineteen cities without anything bad happening to him. Wow! He'd shown America. You see, that's the problem with white America (I'm not talking about Upski specifically). Whites always feel that there's a challenge, that they have to beat the odds, that if they do something nobody else has done they've proved something! But in actuality, what happens is that it's a self experience, their own revelation in how they've perceived change, action, encounter, or a proven point; that often no one literally cares about, but themselves. And what if some of the residents of these ghettos had kicked Upski's ass? Wouldn't he have deserved it? Walking around a ghetto all night is simply asking to be attacked.

"I was sitting along a curb saying, 'C'mon, serial killer, come get me.'" States Upski. What the fuck? That's like saying, "I can't get hooked on drugs, watch this," and putting a glass pipe filled with crack to your mouth!

We're not doing the right things in America to combat the problems; we're simply playing with them. There were three reasons why no one messed in the ghetto with Upski:

1. They thought he was a hype shopping for rocks, or just poor (he walked around with a backpack and never dressed flashy).
2. They may have thought he was 5.0 (undercover cop).
3. He didn't pose a threat, he was always by himself, and nobody wanted to catch a case for whoopin' a white dude. Why bother? Who the fuck cared? He was probably lost or some shit.

Ironically, if the opposite had happened, Upski would have accomplished his goal with far more media coverage and woken up Americans! I bet Upski could have had some financial results if, in the ghetto of every city he went to, he had gotten his ass kicked multiple times, If he had simply had the shit beat out of him, been jacked by women, too; been in and out of the hospital—until the hoods couldn't wait for him to come, until the police had to escort him in and out, and they still kicked his ass! Do you see where I'm going with this? The ghettos will continue to be bad, but for those who are struggling from within. America would have freaked out if they had seen what they (subconsciously) expected to see. A lot of times, a white person isn't real to those in the ghetto—simply an irrelevancy—and that's how Upski was perceived.

So the next time a white person attempts to save the world, try going into a therapeutic rehab where people have been shot multiple times and need help and encouragement to walk again; go to a special needs center where mentally challenged black and white kids need help eating; go to a homeless shelter and help organize whatever the hell needs to be done. Don't use your personal experience to say what's hot and what's not. You needed your ass kicked.

* People's backgrounds, surroundings, and makeup reflect the religion and structure they usually decide upon. Businessmen who are well organized usually pick Catholicism or a Christian denomination that has structure (along with a church) to add to their disciplined lives. Can you imagine a well-established, white-collar yuppie (male or female) going to an all-black Baptist church and jumping around with the Holy Ghost? Or a brother from the hood sitting in a Pentecostal service, or attending a Quaker church, with its silent yet disciplined program? It simply doesn't happen—although I would like to see it, if only because I feel it is important for people to get their hands dirty by experiencing what others do. Sadly, I know it's asking too much; and this yet adds to segregation, when people continue to deal with only those of their race, from their community, or those with a similar plight—even in religion! But what's the main theme that all these people share? Faith. No matter what name you give God, how you worship, or to what extent, you still seek faith. So in "believing," you keep the door open to the possibility of something—the same as believing in your daughter, a promotion, or a car starting in the winter! It's a universal spark that invisibly unites all of us (no matter how big or small) of positive belief that makes you want it to be.

* As Americans, one of our simplest problems is that we get bored quickly. When we get used to seeing things over a period of time, they no longer excite us, they become the norm—even the little things.

Let's take spankings, for instance. Although many Americans don't admit to spanking, they do, and blacks don't spank, they whoop. This has trickled into the white community as well, and many whites are gradually getting tired of spankings (basically love taps) and are progressing to whoopings.

Switching to visual effects, if we were to see black men—all along—in suits and ties (as whites have been shown in movies, commercials, ads, and everyday living), it would become normal to us, tired. After a while, everything becomes boring. That's why blacks wearing suits **stand out, get noticed,** and **catch our eyes**—because it's a refreshing visual.

This is probably why whites are viewed by other races as rigid, because as soon as you hear or think about upper-class whites, you immediately think of stern white men in suits: stiff, with no charm or flexibility.

This also may be why some black women shy away from white men. When they think of or see white men at work, the black women are intimidated by the stiffness they perceive them to have. Again, because we're so used to seeing something, our minds create a false connection. If something becomes the norm to you, just think before you insinuate, figure out how it's lasted so long, and don't be scared to feel comfortable in longevity. (Meaning, don't get bored with repeated people, places and things as long as the outcome is positive and or productive.)

* Real issues with man should be progressing past primitive ideologies, the biggest being that science and God are two separate entities, because they are not! This is the biggest misconception that **the powers that be** and **the church** have put forth. This being so classifies the issue and subtopic of race as humorous and meaningless. What we perceive as racial identity is simply based on inaccuracies and our perception toward these, instead of on facts. Man has much to learn about self, and his literal connection to the one source.

* Brothers in the hood have a big problem being seen with their females. When crack hit the ghetto, along with it came dilemmas and chaos that affected people's actions and emotions. It has become a sign of weakness to show affection publicly to a female. Brothers outside of the hood don't have as bad a problem with this.

In the hood, the only time you see a brother with a female is if they are going to the car. It's acceptable to walk with your female if you have the kids with you and if you're helping her carry something.

And if you see a younger couple walking through the ghetto (and people know they are a couple), the man will be in front, and the female will be trailing about five feet behind him! I'm not talking all couples, only those from the age of sixteen to thirty. And as sad as it is to say, many times the reason that the female is walking behind her man is because she's carrying his gun.

* I remember being mentally burnt out from gymnastics when I was younger. I was too young to take it seriously, but that's what was happening. Meet after meet, competition after competition, I couldn't have any fun because everything was so serious and I was stressed. Yes, I was young, and sure, there were good times when I was "winning" (or at gymnastic camp, with the females), but other than that, it was do or die.

My father, who was quite proud of my gymnastic achievements, was the sole reason for the length of time I participated in it. His pride was enough for me. But it was only a matter of time, and when I finally quit, he was furious and I was hurt. At the time, feeling hurt by disappointing him, I could have chosen to run—to just leave, as many teens do. This issue of my quitting gymnastics was one of the hardest decisions I've made **in my life** because of the love I have for him. I did want to run; and eventually did. (However, not because of the gymnastics incident, but because of the build up of self disappointment; I had such a hard time reaching out, and before I knew it, I had distanced myself from everyone including my parents.)

Families that are still together nowadays have so much to be thankful for.

My problem is with the pressure that parents put on their children, to do what will make them (the parents) happy.

Since American families are assets to our growth and stability, we need to focus on their separation. What makes the family crumble? And not just the parents' situation; the children are products of the domino effect, whether positive or negative.

As a youth, when gymnastics began making me unhappy, I felt that I had the right to voice my concern. The pressure on children from parents is both mental and emotional. If children are close enough to their parents that they actually care what their parents think, or how they may view a situation, that's a good thing. I urge the families that are still together to remember this, because the only ones who can tear your family apart are you.

* Upski's book will never reach the ghetto like he wants, and my book will never reach white upper-class America like I'd like. People ask me daily, "Why do you care so much? Why do you do the things that you do?" And my reply is, "Why don't you?"

As Americans, we tend to put off the job on others. If we see something wrong, we often wait for a collective, or until it's unbearable, before we say something. Why? If I'm out here making it my business to get involved in not only speaking out for my concerns, but yours, your neighbors', and our country's, then let me! And if you're prejudiced and don't feel the way I do, then start your own movement, but don't waste your energy hating mine.

Upski once told me that I was ahead of my time. And when I thought about that, it saddened me. What does that mean? What should it mean? To me, it only means that many people aren't ready for change. The problem is, not only should they be, but they need to be. If we as a country have made mistakes, why aren't we learning from them? Regarding the white-collar citizens who won't read my book, is this because they feel it's not time yet, or because it is inappropriate to their standards? And are the ghetto youth unwilling to read Upski's book because he can't possibly feel like they do?

If Upski and I are making positive changes (no matter how major or minor), along with thousands of others that see these problems—then let us!

* I have a problem with mainstream American society and television networks, and how the two deal with and view racism when they decide to tackle it through sitcoms. Sitcoms come with a safety net, because if the exploitation is demeaning, it's looked upon as humor, and if it's powerful, it's looked upon as a skillful piece of work that the network pulled off.

* I have a problem with cultures and how they perceive white culture. Everyone else seems to have a culture, but when it boils down to white culture, everyone is supposed to know it because we were brought up in school on it, read about it, went on field trips, etc. This makes it hard on whites, because we feel that we're being racist if we embrace our culture because it's so widespread. Too, people need to realize that there are so many subdivisions of white culture: Irish, German, French, Polish, British, etc., and each comes with its own heritage and beliefs.

It gets tricky with white culture, because presently whites may be the majority, although this may alter in years to come. It's because of this that it's accepted as history, and the two get interwoven—history and culture. Because white culture is predominantly what's taught as Americanism, it (at this point) cannot enjoy its individuality. When the day comes when whites are the minority, then the authenticity of the culture will flourish. So why wait? Cultures have to realize that cultural pride is simply about self pride.

* I have a problem with what I call a "Tough Situation." This is when a predicament unfairly finds you and gets awkward, based on a stereotype. For instance, say you're a white hip-hop producer who grew up in the ghetto and has produced tracks for Snoop Doggy Dog, Nas, and Scarface. You walk into a black lounge in Harlem, wanting to relax, get a drink, and enjoy yourself before going to work in the morning (you're doing a joint project with Russell Simmons). But all you get are mean looks and the cold shoulder, even from the bartender, because of how they're used to picturing white people.

Or say that you're a black cowboy from Richmond and on your way home, and your truck breaks down two towns away. You walk into the nearest diner to use the phone and grab a bite to eat. Although you are an authentic cowboy, and your entire town knows you, nobody here has ever seen you. So they stare, snicker, and even point, making you reevaluate your entire life in a split second. These people have never seen a black cowboy, and their bewilderment seems ignorant, which makes you uncomfortable. After using the phone, you don't want to eat in this place, so you go wait in your truck for help to arrive.

In both cases, the person has been placed in a "tough situation" because of their complexion. Even though each was quite representative of the crowd in the bar and diner, they got the cold shoulder. Since we (the majority of America) are usually the ones doing the staring at those that stand out, let's be more mature and open as real people; it shows our individuality.

* I realize that many of the stories, issues, and situations in this book seem harsh, but they are real—real people, real places, and most of all, real life. These are problems in our country that we need to address. Some of you live in the suburbs, some further out, and some in places where these topics and situations seem laughable. Please don't laugh,

because it's your area that people are watching; it's the quiet areas that people are looking to move to, that the government is placing minorities in subsidized housing and section 8; to seemingly invade.

One of the main reasons this book was written, was so that we can look at and handle these problems. Running from this problem is building more prisons; running from this problem is keeping drugs in the ghetto; and most of all, running is neglect—to not want to deal with it as it increasingly gets worse!

This book is not to freak you out, as you sit in your quiet little domain reading it, but to wake you up. Realize that people are out here in the field daily, combating these problems, and need your help. Really! Involvement comes from all walks of life.

* Much of your perception of this book and of life is guided by your faith and religion. Regardless of what religion you are, you've got to put faith in man. It's important. Because although you may feel alone, there are others that feel exactly the way you do. Exactly. Putting a little faith in man shows that you trust self, or you wouldn't do so. I realize that this may be hard to swallow for those who are strongly religious, since you have been taught to trust God and put all faith in him, and him only. But remember that man is of God, and God works through man. Just trust a little more that we can pull this together, because we can, and I know we can.

The problem that we have is that not many of us realize what a huge revelation it is for each and every one of us to be here. Everyone; from the hungry in Ethiopia to the crack babies here in America. Creation, fate, God, science, or however you perceive it, your existence has been materialized into your being you. And though you may feel that your situation is not meaningful at times, it is. All is connected. And the concept of **being** is so immense that it is simple—we are here, all of us; so let us prosper, all of us.

FREEDOM

(HOUSE ARREST)

As I mentioned earlier, I have gone through a lot while writing this book. During the Adrenaline chapter, I was on house arrest in Cabrini. Now, nearly five years later, I'm on house arrest in Humboldt Park—another buck-wild neighborhood down the street from Cabrini. (In fact, as I'm writing this, someone just got shot five times in front of my house, so I'm running back and forth to the window to see what's happening—I'll keep you posted—nothing is gonna stop me from finishing this book!)

Cook County Jail is overcrowded, so Monday through Friday (around 10:00 a.m.) they offer inmates with a bond of ten thousand or less a program entitled **Electronic Monitoring**—or, as we call it, house arrest. All you need is a legal place to go. But getting picked for house arrest is only the beginning of a thorough six-stage process in making it to your home, and staying there. Believe that!

First of all, in getting to the house arrest location (in Cook County Jail), you have to travel three blocks or a little less, depending on where you are. There are fourteen divisions in the county, all connected underground by tunnels except Division 11, where you will be transported by van. The problem with this lengthy walk is that it gives the guards time to provoke you; meaning, they don't give a damn if you get house arrest or not, so they often talk crap and try to pull you off your square so that they can send you back upstairs. Just hope that you make it past the initial **walk to** house arrest.

Second, once you get to the house arrest location, you are literally pushed into a fenced cage (one of two) that will be your new domain for the next eight hours! And the yelling begins. The tension increases. You have eight hours to get in touch with your people to make it home. Easier said than done. You are given a pencil and a form to fill out—the name and number of your first choice of where you would like to go. The investigator will call the number on the form to confirm. If no confirmation is made, you will have to hit the phone yourself, frantically trying other options of someone to accept you. Remember, this is during business hours, so your wife, girlfriend, or parents (or whomever you live with) will most likely be at work, and they will have to be contacted. If these people are not contacted (and confirmed) by 7:00 p.m., you will have to go back upstairs (losing your lottery ticket) and suffer with the rest of the inmates. Time is running out.

There are seven phones by the cage. These phones will be in constant use throughout the day, and when the guards (who insist that you call them "investigators") tell you to get off the phone, **you had better!** Your goal is to make contact with your people and let them know that the investigator is about to call them to verify your acceptance. (And if you can't get through to one number—keep going!)

Third comes elimination. There are **two** cages, and since you are in one cage, all the people who the investigator makes contact with (verifying their acceptance) get called out to go to the **other** cage. This is the lucky cage—the one that is a step closer to going home. You can only pray that your name is called. But it won't be. It never is. In fact, of the one hundred of you that are in the first cage, only five to ten get called to go to the lucky cage (during this first round). Which means it's going to be a long day with a lot of phone revolving!

Elimination comes in different forms—obstacles. Not only are you trying to get to the lucky cage, but you are faced with obstacles in trying to get there.

1. There is supposed to be no talking, which is literally impossible, and the investigators know it. So quiet talk is acceptable, but it never remains quiet! Thus, the investigator hollers and singles out the loudest person, sending him to a bench on the side of the cage—he'll be going back upstairs. Damn, so close to freedom!

2. You only have five minutes per call once you get to a phone; and though you will be able to get back on (many times throughout the day), you had better get off when the investigator tells you to do so—or you'll end up on the bench. Damn, so close to freedom!

3. Cook County Jail is co-ed. The women also getting house arrest will be twenty feet away from you, blowing kisses and

mouthing their phone numbers. Do not, I repeat, do not, get caught talking to them! Someone always gets caught, and the bench keeps filling. Damn, so close to freedom!

Elimination has one more major obstacle that will affect you during the day (whether or not you make it to the lucky cage), and that's how the investigators talk to you. To many, this may sound easy, but to the majority (including myself), this will be the hardest obstacle of all! Really. Because it is constant, from the **walk to** house arrest, up until you make it home—if you make it—the investigators literally holler at you like you are a piece of crap. Now, I'm the first to admit that your goal is to not say anything back, because you want to make it home, of course. Just ignore them, right? Easier said than done. Seriously. We are talking about men (investigators) who far surpass the hollering stage; they will threaten you, physically push you, and disrespect your family members.

"Man, I don't give a fuck because you're talking to your sick grandma, fuck you and that bitch, hang up my phone!" (And the investigator snatches the phone and hangs it up, waiting for you to do something.)

"And fuck you, white boys! I don't give a fuck about you down here, you don't run shit! Say one word and I'll smack the shit out of you!" (And the investigator pushes one of the white men toward the wall, and he falls into someone else,)

"And you niggas that think you hard—what's up? We can go right here! C'mon, li'l bitch, I want the biggest man in here to say something, I'm gonna show aye what I got!" (And the investigator steps to someone, knocking his hat out of his hand and waiting for him to say something or swing.)

Yes, from disrespectful slurs to racial put-downs—not to mention physical contact—these investigators will cross the line. Be ready!

Okay, fourth; you've been approved, you've moved to the lucky cage, you've gotten your house arrest box and your house arrest band, and you're eager to go home. But now, to your disgust, comes the **standing game**. This is when the majority is in the lucky cage and the investigator continues to push his authority by making everyone suffer because of one man—who was simply talking at the same level as everyone; meaning, there is no one man!

"Okay, whoever is talking loud just ruined it for everyone! Get on your fuckin' feet now and face the wall! Everyone! Stand there for the next two hours with your box in your hand! I better not catch you setting it down!" (And while he's yelling, he's running into the cage and literally pushing everyone—young and old—into the wall. It's crazy.)

So there you, are standing on your feet, with the house arrest box in your hands, your legs and arms are sore, and you're literally half an inch from the man in front of you, as is the man directly behind you. Everyone can smell each other's funk and is wishing this day was over, when suddenly, the investigator hollers at everyone to turn around and watch a movie explaining the procedures concerning house arrest—the do's and don'ts. (Another hour on your feet because it's in both English **and** Spanish!) So, by the time you go and get the house arrest band actually strapped around your ankle, you feel like collapsing. (However, I've seen overweight men collapse—not because their legs gave out, but because their ankles were too fat for the house arrest band to be placed on them—and they fainted from panic! Really.)

Now, fifth, comes the long ride home, if you make it. Yes! But it's not over, because the fifth stage has backfired on many men:

1. You are not allowed to give any directions to your house (whether you live on a one-way street, in a back apartment, on a dead-end street, in a skyscraper, or on the moon). It is considered an insult to the investigators, who have driven all around Chicago doing their job—which they will let you know, over and over and over. And yet, there is always that dumbass who still insists on giving directions, because he's so frantic to get home—and never gets there because he can't keep his mouth shut!

2. Once you get to your residence, you're praying that your house arrest box works! Can you imagine? You've made it through the whole day, you've overcome all the obstacles, and by some cruel twist of fate, the box that they gave you has a malfunction and isn't working properly. It's the worst sight in the world to see someone get out of the van with the investigator, be in his own home for about twenty minutes, and have to return with the investigator! Damn, so close to freedom! (He'll have to go through the whole thing all over again the next day, and pray that the new box works!)

Sixth, and last, is beating the stress and tension once you actually make it home and the investigator leaves. Man, for real! Because you are only allowed 100 feet to get around your house, and that's not far. But you are free! Right? **Right!** Well, it's all perception, because that momentary feeling of freedom wears off quick—real quick! And the moment it wears off (which sometimes is twenty minutes after the investigator leaves), the tension builds up—it's unbearable! In fact, I've seen guys get home and literally leave out the back door the moment the investigator leaves out the front! Can you imagine being confined to the literal circumference of your home or apartment—all the time, not even being able to check your mailbox? There have been times when I've felt like a little kid, looking out the window and seeing my guys, but not being able to go out and play. It's crazy. Then there's the stress of the electric band around your ankle. Taking a shower or a bath causes anxiety. They say it can get wet, but every time it does you get paranoid, thinking that water somehow leaked inside the band, and that they're on their way to get you! Day after day, you wake up with the band still attached, and day after day, you go from one side of your house to the other. The days that you get to go to court (usually once a month) feel like freedom to your soul! And you dread going back to your own home. Now, depending on how your court case is coming along, there will be days when the tension and stress is so high that you almost give up and start planning on where you'll go once you break out. But you have to keep reminding yourself that being in your own home is way better than being locked down in the county jail. The level of freedom is higher. Isn't that weird, the **level** of freedom?

A few paragraphs ago (the fifth stage), I focused on the obstacles in riding home, but what I didn't mention, only because the momentum was elsewhere, was the incredible feeling of freedom that overcomes you upon leaving the county jail, which ironically dissipates in your own home soon after. Can you imagine? Here you are, feeling on top of the world, going to the comfort of your own home (that, too, is probably a strong reason why some men give directions to the investigators when they're not supposed to—because they're so overwhelmed by the new level of freedom that they can't restrain themselves), when suddenly, that feeling of freedom is crushed by a new perception!

So here's the catch: what does freedom mean to you? While you're at work, is it your lunch break? Is it spending time with your kids at the park? Is it walking barefoot in the sand at the beach? Or how about taking a hot bubble bath while nobody's home? Maybe payday on Friday, at the bar with a drink? Maybe on a plane leaving the country? However you perceive freedom is actually an analysis of situation and self. The levels of freedom are controlled by you.

Your physical presence on this planet is actually driven by spiritual freedom. However, don't think for one moment that physical death is the ultimate stage and the release (or accomplishment) of freedom. It is not; it is simply the end of your physical stage here. Your goal is to pursue physical freedom and to create the balance needed to connect with self.

To recap the shooting incident in front of my apartment: Well, dude was a **Cobra** (Latino street organization riding under the six-point star), and there was a beef with the **Maniacs**, another predominantly Latino organization under the six-point. They were at war, and dude supposedly went through their hood during war time, so they let loose the cannons on him. He died on the corner of Maplewood and Potomac. May he rest in peace. He was eighteen.

***

(Taking out the Garbage)

Looking back on the hard chapters of my life and the moments of freedom that were offered (or that I had to create), one unique incident stands out.

It was about 11:00 p.m. and I was in the penitentiary, taking out the garbage! I was allowed to leave my block (building) and walk a hundred feet, unattended, to the dumpster. That hundred feet to the dumpster and back was my most memorable time in the penitentiary...

Leaving the block, whether winter or summer, allowed me peace of mind. I would walk as slowly as possible, and a thousand and one things raced my mind. This was my closest thing to freedom, and—in a weird way—was freedom! I was outside, under the stars, unattended, in the middle of what appeared to be nowhere (cornfields to the left and right; all penitentiaries are in rural areas), it was night, and the fresh air eased my lonely soul. I could make it. Yes, these precious hundred-foot walks, offered to me through my job as a porter, kept alive a glimmer of hope that I would make it home. That I had a home.

As I threw the large bags over the top of the dumpster, I awaited the pounding noise the bag would make once it hit the bottom, or the smacking sound it would make hitting another garbage sack. The sound would break the spell, and remind me that this moment was over; I had to return to the walls, cells, and hatred that surrounded me, continuously, always surrounding me.

I longed for the nights, that cool air, that time to be me again, by myself, my ten minutes of freedom, as I took out the garbage.

(THE TRIP HOME)

When you are in the penitentiary, the night before going home is the longest night of your life. The minutes counting down, anticipation, seclusion, and the threat of freedom; meaning, the actual realization that tomorrow (at this same time) you'll be back in society, enjoying privacy, with no group of onlookers, no direct orders, no shanks, no walls, and no inner pain of losing supposed time! (And, of course, sex.) Tomorrow, at this time, you'll be free.

My last night in the penitentiary, I fed the entire deck, had a grab bag, and held a spade and poker tournament. All bid farewell.

Bang! Bang! went my cell door as the guard hit it obnoxiously to wake me up at 4:00 a.m. My celly said goodbye as I grabbed my bag. I looked at the guard and I could tell that he didn't want me to leave. He was set in the fact that I had helped keep the peace in my block of the penitentiary. All the problems that they had, they could call me! Whenever. And the problem would be fixed. Still, he too was anxious for me to begin my journey, because I deserved it.

I was escorted to the front **visitation** room, where we (the seven inmates that were going home) were to change into our "dress out" clothes. We were then fingerprinted (because, contrary to what the system wants you to believe, human fingerprints do actually alter slightly over time; so we were often fingerprinted during our stay, and of course upon leaving), had our last mug shot taken (which will be publicly displayed on the Internet), and taken to the front gate. There we were to board the **Blue Bird, Grey Goose,** or—as you guys plainly state—the prison bus.

Boarding the bus, still in handcuffs (always being handcuffed, for any type of movement, even upon release), we were driven to the Greyhound bus terminal in the closest town. I looked around and felt lonely. Nobody knew what I had been through. Not just the gangster shit, but the real things that make a man a real man: standing his ground, dealing with isolation, studying in spite of major distractions, missing loved ones' funerals, holidays and birthdays, and having to deal with hardcore personalities, including cellmates. The guards monitored us as we got on the bus. This was their job, to stay and wait until the bus was out of sight, so the inmates would not explore or become a threat to the small town. Hence, they hawked us until the bus rolled away from a memorable life episode. No more prison guards!

Automatically, you feel that the others on the bus somehow know that you were just released. They don't, but this feeling will follow you for months as you reenter into society.

I went to the middle of the bus and looked around. There was a girl with an open seat beside her, so I sat next to her. She looked good (even familiar), so I started talking to her. Astonishingly, not only had we briefly gone to the same high school, but we went together (dated) for a whole summer—nine years ago!

Since all the penitentiaries in Illinois are strategically located in the most rural areas ever conceived, it definitely gives you time to think. And think you will: How am I going to get my money? Man, I can't wait to eat real food tonight! Who am I going to see tonight? Who's tippin' on the block now? I gotta call my parole officer! I gotta get some condoms ASAP!

Then the realization hits you, as you pass barns, cows, and cornfields—you are actually leaving! You then automatically think about those you left behind; all the real guys that you bonded with, real men that stood on the front line—those who were honestly railroaded by the system but had gotten over it through time! Those men would die in the penitentiary—literally having fifty or more years left to do. These were the real men who still offered advice, even though they'd lost their freedom. And you wanted to release these caged birds.

There were five stops before Chicago, and my former girlfriend had two stops left. She and I exchanged numbers before she got off, and I got my first kiss as a free man. However, though I had actually bumped into an old girlfriend (coming fresh out of the penitentiary), and though we seemed to be talking ninety miles a minute, my mind was racing with anticipation elsewhere. I couldn't wait to get back to Chicago. And before I knew it, the seven of us were standing up and looking out the windows at the Chicago skyline. (We literally couldn't stay seated.) All in awe. We had made it.

Our first stop in Chicago was the 95th Street bus terminal, and surprisingly, the other six men all started to grab their belongings. All six were paroling to the South Side! We showed love and bid each other farewell. And though the bus was still full, I was by myself.

Looking out the window, I now noticed people instead of the city. I had been gone two and a half years—straight—after receiving a seven-year sentence. In those few years, much had changed in clothing styles, hair, and jewelry. When I left people were wearing gold links, now they were wearing wannabe platinum—silver. When I left, people were wearing Karl Kani, FUBU, and Mecca; now they were wearing Sean John, Enyce, and Girbaud. Girls had gone from wearing nose rings to wearing eyebrow rings and tongue rings; recently, the girls in Chicago went back to nose rings, but as a symbol of lesbianism. I noticed that many of the white women now had big assess like the sistas, and many of the white men dressed like the street brothas.

As the bus pulled into the downtown Greyhound bus terminal, I was ready. I accepted the challenge of getting things back on track. My goal was to continue my Chicago destiny: bringing my book out, continuing my spoken word career and lyricist careers, speaking to students and gang members, and continuing my community activism—not just in Cabrini, but citywide. Yes, my hands were full!

At the Greyhound terminal on Harrison, I grabbed my belongings. I felt both free and awkward, but I knew that the free feeling wouldn't last long.

The feeling of being released from the penitentiary is actually difficult to describe. (Bear in mind that incarcerated men have to be locked up for more than one year to qualify for this scenario.) Many a writer has given a personal description; however, freedom from the penitentiary can only be described as a numbness of the whole, as a new reality chapter that literally blows you away. The individual will experience it as an unfolding occurrence of actions in separate waves—waves that seem to surprise you and yet remind you of freedom, the waves whisper that yes, you are free. You really are. And then they'll remind you of the penitentiary and its schedules and order, which will remind you that you may be only temporarily free. It's up to the individual to overcome the institutionalized perception.

Again, freedom is ascertained by self...

Freedom is ascertained by self!

WHY IS IT?

Take a deep breath and ponder sometimes. Think about what is really taking place in a situation. Think about it. Feel it. Some of the following "why is it" questions are fun, some are deep, and some will make you stop and think—and think some more, because you're supposed to.

As always, we'll look at these problems in hopes of analyzing them and finding solutions. Americans are good at reading between the lines, it's what we do. So continue doing so, continue searching and asking yourself—why is it?

* Why is it that in the school cafeteria everyone sits in their own racial huddle?

* Why is it that people think that more blacks are on welfare (financial aid) than whites?

* Why is it that the bad cops fuck it up for the good cops?

* Why is it that you're now apparently over the hill at thirty, instead of at fifty?

* Why is it that some black men consider white men with blue eyes to be of the devil—but not women with blue eyes?

* Why is it that no one from the urban area ever wins the big lottery?

* Why is it that *In Living Color*, *New York Undercover*, and *South Central* were taken off the air?

* Why is it that the majority of high schools need metal detectors?

* Why is it that the recidivism rate increases each year?

* Why is it that Rosa Parks did so much for a good cause, yet the first place black youth go is to the back of the bus?

* Why is it that brothers have to die in order to get respect?

* Why is it that when you're locked up the officers talk big shit to you, sometimes rough you up and make your predicament hell, but as soon as you get out and run into them on the street, they're as quiet as a church mouse?

* Why is it that many of us are sad on holidays, when we should be happy?

* Why is it that racist whites are usually trailer-park trash?

* Why is it that some black women talk shit about white women and how they live, then turn right around and watch the soap operas?

* Why is it that cops have a vision when they join the force, but it dies out within the first two years?

* Why is it that rap music is considered Hip Hop by mainstream society?

* Why is it that the differences between races are looked upon as being physical when they are simply mental?

* Why is it that kids run away from home so young, and their parents can't figure out why?

* Why is it that bothers in the county jail lie and say they have a paid lawyer?

* Why is it that Tupac and Biggie keep coming out with shit?

* Why is it that, if you don't have a baby by the age of twenty nowadays, there is a misconception that you obviously can't have kids?

* Why is it that many brothers on the streets are out there bad (getting high off that shit), but as soon as they get locked up they wanna be plugged and criticize others?

* Why is it that many black men and women suck in their lips when they are around white people?

* Why is it that "big and beautiful" is always "in" for fat people until they lose some weight, and then they too want to help other fat people lose weight?

* Why is it that white people have no problem getting their phone number listed in the yellow pages, but as soon as a brotha gets his phone cut on, he doesn't want it to be listed?

* Why is it that portions of the original bible are excluded?

* Why is it that major supermarkets throw food away daily, but when a homeless person tries to get it out of the garbage, the cops try and lock them up?

* Why is it that racist whites think that blacks want to be white?

* Why is it that when playing "cops and robbers" kids don't want to be the cops anymore?

* Why is it that we as Americans think we have it so hard?

* Why is it that we know AIDS is killing people, yet we don't use condoms?

* Why is it that when you're locked up, your women breaks bad before your trial is even finished?

* Why is it that artists have to die in order to become famous?

* Why is it that we feel the grass is greener on the other side?

* Why is it that when you're in a gang, your boys will tell you they got your back, forever, no matter what—but they leave out the part about you ever getting locked up?

* Why is it that top notch scientists believe in God?

* Why is it that Christmas commercials now come on before Halloween?

* Why is it that Tiger Woods is black to black people, but oriental to some white people?

* Why is it that in the future, racial issues will be so obsolete that people won't even talk about them anymore, yet right now we're scared to talk about them? Hello?

* Why is it that the mixed babies of an interracial couple look so beautiful?

OUTCOME

* "Just a little, at that last moment, is all it takes." K-So 7-13-00

When I was nine years old, I met a boy who would end up becoming my best friend. He was the same age as me, white, and poor. For four straight years we were inseparable, and came to know each other like the back of our hands. The summer before eighth grade, he moved. Two years later, out of the blue, I received a phone call from him. Not only was I shocked, but I felt disrespected and saddened by what he had to say.

My erstwhile best friend gave me some off-the-wall garbage about distancing himself from all minorities, and criticized me for being one, talking like one, even acting like one—though he hadn't seen me in two years! Then he went on to say that he hated minorities because they all acted ignorant, childish, and phony. Before we hung up, he made it quite clear that he was going to do something about it, as if he was on some evangelical shit—although he had just mentioned distancing himself. What? Exactly.

I didn't hear from him for many years after that. When I finally did, it was through a mutual friend. I now had a number to call my former best friend, who really wanted to hear from me. But the more I thought about it, the more I didn't want to contact him, because of how we'd left off. So I didn't.

A year went by, and during that time more than five different people came to me with the same message about contacting my former best friend. Since we were now adults (just hitting twenty-one), I knew that I would straight snap on him if he started with the racism BS. But the more I thought about it, the more I wanted to call—to check his ass. So I called.

After I got off the phone with him, I felt good, not because I had checked him, but because I didn't have to. It turned out that my erstwhile best friend not only apologized for being the negative crank he'd been, but said that he'd realized his ignorance had come from not truly knowing what he had been talking about and criticizing! He'd taken his bad experiences with minorities and redirected his former idealism—and now, once he had gotten to know some minorities, he felt foolish. In fact, his new girlfriend was Latino, one of his close friends was black, and his onetime best friend had finally called—and he wanted me to be a part of his new life! I proudly accepted.

My former best friend is again in my life, and though we are working to better our friendship as adults, I'm proud of him crossing the bridge on his own. He got married to his girlfriend two months ago...

As the years roll by us and time seems to slip, so do the once solid ideas, motives, and inspirations of our lives. How we grow mentally is simply a reflection of what we've absorbed, who we've absorbed it from, and how we've absorbed it. People make mistakes by getting dead set on a subject that they feel can be one-sided, and often, as time passes, the energy spent on proving your point seems wasted. We make big deals out of what we feel our life revolves around, when often it doesn't. Nor do we fully understand what we claim to believe in. What do we believe in? What do we really believe in?

This book straddles the fence from the streets to the upper classes. One of the vital ideas to grasp from this book is balance. It helps you become the human that is needed at this point in our development. Financial status somehow manages to create a blind ego that makes it difficult to truly accept the reality of others' finances—the haves don't understand the detailed struggles of the have nots, and vice versa. What balance does is invisibly subdue the ego so that fairness can be perceived in both realities.

Though I often feel I have something to say, when I look around—at the depth of life, people, nature, the universe, and where I stand in it—I think that my words are frivolous. And when this happens, I continue crossing my own bridge. I look at people and I want to know them. I want to know: What's the most influential thing you've ever done? How long will our summers be summers before they are winters? And what makes emotions so hard to handle when they're inside our bodies, which we supposedly control?

The fact remains that there are millions of people who simply get along with other human beings of all races, because their gut instincts tell them that these members of other races are just human beings.

I will say that there are no secret plans that we can uncover, but we can better ourselves, which in turn betters how we act toward others. How each one of us leaves this planet is a true indication of who we truly are. Soon each one of us will leave; it will be here before we know it. There are so many things, other than race relations, to be worried about.

Realize as you walk down the street that everyone is affected by mass perception, governmental decisions, and you—yes, you. Your actions actually do have a domino effect on others, and vice versa. Other people's lives may seem insignificant: possibly because they don't look like you, don't make as much money as you do, make much more money than you do, or their morals seem less developed than yours. Regardless, get over it! We are all affected, we all deserve respect, and we're more alike than we think, perceive, or give credit to.

I've had sad and wonderful times writing this book, because I've seen how petty many of us are, yet how truly forceful we can be if we come together. I know there now seem to be all these new avenues to think of, but just remember, they're not new. They were there all along; we've just tapped into them and progressed in how we think about them. In the next couple of years, Americans will have tackled and absorbed much of this, like a new language. It might take a moment to catch on, but we will.

This book is designed to simply be a road map to connect people, cultures, and ideas. Hopefully, there will be more like it that we can absorb and pass on, physically and mentally, to our youth. They deserve it.

There are also many books by powerful, diverse writers of all nationalities that are already out there and deserve our full attention. Please do your homework and seek these treasures.

The bottom line is that we're here now, and four hundred years from now we may not be. Not because of a racial war (because, to tell you the truth, this will never happen—too many people are waking up and having mixed relationships, children, and families), but because of all the other real issues that are threatening the Earth: nuclear war, global warming, flooding, famine, disease, pollution, etc.

Now, jump light-years ahead and picture an entirely different concept of planet Earth, its people, and what we've manifested. Though our technology can become as advanced as we let it, make it, and want it, our human spirits will still seek the same attention—to be loved, wanted, respected, connected, and have a feeling of belonging. This will never change because we are of God and the universe, and we do belong. We do.

Today, we are faced with the circumstances, issues, and problems I bring to light in this book. One day I would like to compare them with those of my great-grandchildren, and yours too. Wouldn't it be nice to know that our great-great-grandchildren won't have to worry about racism? Well, it starts now.

It is also important for you to remember that there is major money in public and media racism. This has secretly been a powerful device of **the powers that be**, and they have capitalized on it for more than two hundred and fifty years! This is true. Don't fall into this media trap.

Einstein once said that "Racism is America's greatest disease." It's sad that one of the world's smartest men, who was not American but came to live in America, stated this observation.

My view of you is that of a partner, because it's me and you against the world! Sometimes, we all think that we don't need each other, but the reality is that you are me, and without you there is no me—and vice versa. Thank you for seeing our world through my eyes.

Love and support,
Pete (K-So) Keller

DEFINITIONS

These definitions are to familiarize you with the everyday street lingo that people use. I want you to think about something, and what I'm about to tell you may surprise you, but it's true. America has a highly over-exaggerated perception of "us," meaning those with money that supposedly represent mainstream America. In actuality, the "us" is simply a smaller percentage of "them." In fact, counting the younger generation (those that the census doesn't poll), the majority of the middle class, the ghetto, and even a percentage of the wealthy do not fall into "the powers that be" interpretation of America, and what it's supposed to represent. They just don't. That's not to say they are ghetto or street, simply hip in their own way, and not blind to the realism that the urban scene has to offer, good or bad.

Many of these words are deeper than just plain street words. They are actually ghetto words, but mainstream ghetto—meaning, throughout America. And though they are real and larger (especially in people's minds) than they've been getting credit for, many are negative. However, the ghetto is often a negative place and we cannot forget this. Thus, the positive link to the bridge is that you are relating to and understanding a concept that some are scared to tackle. Hat's off to you.

AA—Abbreviation for "Aid and Assist." In most cases, it's used in helping someone fight, to assist them in their endeavors.

Animation—Style of dance where the body seems to move from frame to frame, related to break dancing; to skillfully vibrate the entire body as if animated.

Bag Up—To put product in the bag of choice when handling narcotics.

Baller—One who is looked upon as having a lot of money and material things. Although some ballers may be legal, the majority are not.

Battle—Reference for break dancing and rap competition. This can also mean all conflicts in friendly competition that are nonviolent.

Biting—When someone copies your style, moves, or lyrics; to imitate without authorization.

Bling Bling—This term came from the sparkle of diamonds and platinum (with diamond cut), and is used to describe someone or something that stands out, shines, and looks good. "Hey, look at Randy in his new platinum Rolex, he's bling blinging!"

Bobo—To "kick the bobo" is a phrase that means talking; a new term for shooting the breeze.

Bogus—Not up to par; for someone's actions to be invalid, as far as your perception of how they should be (disrespectful, phony, obnoxious, rude, or mean). Bogus can also mean a place or a thing not being representative of what it's supposed to be. "Check out Johnny's car with all those scratches; he must have had an accident, his shit looks bogus now!"

Bomb—1. Something good; something you crave, want, admire, or that appeals to you. "That new movie *Matrix 4* is the bomb." 2. To draw graffiti on a place or thing.

Booster—One who steals to support their drug habit.

Booty Call—Someone you can call for sex; the act of arranging sexual plans. "I got a seven p.m. booty call with Jill, and a ten p.m. boot call with Cheryl."

Brainstorming—To instantly make up a rhyme as it comes out; used in slamming or rapping.

Break Bad—Used when talking about your wife or girlfriend not dealing with you anymore once you're locked up. "Man, dog, Laura broke bad on me, I just received a Dear John letter."

Buckin'—When someone goes out of their way to get a spot, place, or function; often used in a negative aspect. "Randy is brownnosing the boss; did you see him buckin' for a new office?"

Buck Rogers—Court date that has been set for a long time away. "Man, this phony-ass judge just gave me a Buck Rogers for two months from now!"

Budda—Marijuana.

Bum-rush—To simply run up on someone, usually done with two or more people. "Get out of my face, ride, before me and my guys bum-rush your ass!"

Burner—1. Term for elaborate graffiti piece. "Did you see that burner on the side of that store? It was phat!" 2. A gun.

Bust— 1. To shoot a gun. 2. To ejaculate.

Bust a Stain—To commit a caper; to have a plan in committing crime for money.

Bust Down—Female who is easily persuaded into sex or oral sex. "What? You said you could see yourself going with who? Lucy! Man, she's a bust down hoe!"

Butter—1. This New York word at first was equivalent to "fresh," but as it hit Chicago, it was given a completely different meaning. Butter refers to the potency of cocaine. If you have the best, strongest, most potent crack on the block, you have butter! 2. Hair. "You need a new perm, G, because your butter is struck!"

Byrd—A kilo of cocaine. "Henry picked up two byrds, so he'll be tight later."

Cap Move—To play it off; to cover up an initial intention with a phony one only to throw someone off, so that you can still achieve your initial intent.

Case—To talk about someone, to crack jokes about them.

Check—To put someone in their place, often verbally. "I had to check Willy yesterday for driving my car without my permission."

Cheddar—Money. "I ain't going to the show, I gotta stack my cheddar today."

Chief—1. To smoke a lot of weed, usually in blunt form. 2. A high-ranking member in a street organization.

Chicken Head—Female with short hair.

Chi Town—Old nickname for Chicago. Now often referred to as the "Go" or "Go Town."

Chuck Hole—The opening in the doors of county jail and penitentiary cells where food can be passed through, without opening the door itself.

Click—The group you hang with.

C-Note—One hundred dollars. "You owe me a C-note, Reggie, pay up!"

Come Up—To achieve something better than what you had; whether it's a better or newer car, more money, or a new girlfriend, it's a come up.

Commissary—When in a county jail or penitentiary, the store you are allowed to go to (if you have money on the books) for food and toiletries.

Crack—Pre-cooked cocaine sold on the street, ready to smoke.

Creeping—To sneak around with another lover or sex partner.

Cut—Song that you like. "You heard that new one by Genuine? That's my cut!"

Deck— Term for the buildings blocks section, day room or gallery where you reside while incarcerated; whether in the County jail or penitentiary. The deck is the entire floor (often with an upper and lower level) where inmates can walk around, go to their cells, get on the phone, use the showers and/or bathroom, and enjoy the dayroom where there is often a Television.

Defense—1. Sex from the male point of view, as far as how he gave it to the female. "I threw the defense on my girl last night; it was on!"

Defense—2. Heroin.

Dip—1. A secret lover on the side; someone who is not your main partner. 2. Old school County Jail meal (not to be confused with penitentiary **Chili Mac**), made with meat, cool aid and chips.

Dirty—1. To have something illegal on your person. "Damn, I can't get pulled over, I'm dirty; I got four dime bags still on me!" 2. Also had a brief run as the equivalent of money.

DL—Abbreviation for "Down Low." To do something on the sneak or undercover, pertaining to a person, place, or thing. Often used when referring to a secret relationship; similar to creeping, but its range is wider. "Hand me those car keys, but do it on the DL because I don't want Cindy to see me leave."

Dope—1. Heroin. 2. Something you like or that appeals to you, equivalent to fresh or butter.

Dub—Twenty dollars.

Dubs—Twenty-inch rims for a car.

Dusties—Title invented by Chicago's very own Herb Kent, for records that were hits at one time and are now old, but will always be cuts to us! "Ooh! Hurry up, turn on the radio, it's old school Sunday and they're playing all the dusties!"

EX—Term for the drug Ecstasy.

Fade—1. When shooting dice, to fade someone is to bet against them; to do this is being known as a fader. 2. Haircut known as bald head fade. 3. Technique DJs use in mixture (on turntables) which brings records in and out by using the cross fader.

False Flag—To not be in a gang yet throw up their symbols; to perpetrate.

Fam- Short term for "Family". Started with the street organizations, and now has been watered down to the equivalence of "homie" or "man". "Where you been fam, i've been waiting two hours!"

Fell Off—For someone or something to lose the standard or status they once had. "Look at Doug over there, that brotha fell off. Remember when he used to have the barber shop and Laundromat? He ain't got shit now!"

Fin—Five dollars; also referred to as a fimp.

Fit—Short for outfit. "I'll be back, I'm gonna go buy a fit for the dance tonight."

Five-O (5.0)—The police.

Flicking—To stand out, shine, or be doing well; also referred to as flossing. "Did you see that platinum link Lucy has? She's flicking."

Folks—As L.A. has the Crips and Bloods, we have Folks and People; Folks being one street organization, People being the other; all other street organizations fall under these two branches.

Foo Fops—For someone to physically beat up someone else. "Man, you should have seen dude right there, he put the foo fops on old boy!"

Foot Soldiers—In the Chicago street organizations of Folks and People, the foot soldiers are at the bottom of the totem pole as far as status.

Foot Work—Dance done in Chicago to house music, mainly with feet movement, when people on the dance floor bust out their best moves. One of our biggest underground house cuts is dedicated to foot work, the song chants "Let me see your foot work, let me see your foot work!"

Friend—Term used when females (usually twenty-one and older) introduce a man they're having sex with. "Hi, Mama, this is my friend, Jerry."

Game—Referred to as "The Game." Used in reference to street activity, hustling, boosting, playerism, banging, and drug selling. One of the most monumental phrases concerning this term is "The Game is cold, but it's fair."

Gear—Clothing.

Ghetto—We all know what the ghetto is; however, when someone is referred to as being "ghetto," it's usually because they sound illiterate, look thuggish, or act out of context for the occasion.

Gone Up—For the deck to "go up" or have "gone up" simply means that gangs have fought and torn up the deck.

Go Getter—One who cannot be stopped in achieving their goal of success in whatever field they pursue.

Go Town—New nickname for Chicago. Taken from the ending (go) of Chicago, it was created from the **go getter** mentality that the Windy City has continued to create; there is nothing Chi (shy) about Chicago.

Graffiti—Hip Hop's terminology for art, which it is. Graffiti to Hip Hop and street culture is not the same concept as to white-collar society. Components of graffiti are tagging, pieces, burners, and throw ups. The different styles of graffiti lettering are bubble, 3-D, animation, futuristic, pipes, thrash, wild style, block, prehistoric, cursive, metal, ice, and space!

G-Shot—Nude pictures, movies, or real life. "Did you see that G-shot Kelly gave Peter on visitation?"

Hater—The supposed opposite of Player; one who you feel dislikes you, jealous or gets in the way of your progress.

Heads—1. The top-ranking members in street organizations (gangs). 2. Hip-hop term for other Hip-hop affiliates. "Yo, it's some heads over there by the bridge doing some phat throw ups!"

Heroin—Instead of giving the elements and makeup of heroin, I feel it's more important to give the street terms. Heroin is now rampant everywhere, including the suburbs, and is increasing. Heroin goes by the following names: smack, dope, blow, Karachi, boy, brown, and China White!

Hip Hop—This concept has now been revised from its former five components to six; see ULON.

Hooch—Wine made while incarcerated.

Hoochie—Street term for whore, someone fast and easy. Other similar terms are: hoodrat, skank, hoe, skoochie mama, trick, bust down, and skeezer.

Hot—For a location or a person to be heavily patrolled or watched by police. "I ain't walking by Sewer Park, that spot's too hot."

House—Cousin of Hip Hop. House music has a following, with clothing, dances, terminology, and style. House music's beats (or RPMs) are anything over 115. Chicago is the capital of House music.

Humbug—To physically fight. "You shoulda seen those two chicken heads humbug yesterday."

Hustling—To achieve your goal by moving fast, beating others to the punch skillfully, powerfully, and determinedly.

Hydro—Short for hydroponics; marijuana that is grown in a specific manner to achieve the best results; sometimes in water, under sunlamps, or in a green house, but always timed. Hydro is the marijuana of choice on the street.

Hype—Someone who's strung out on cocaine; a dope fiend.

Izo Izang—Form of street speech where "izo" and "kizo" replace the white version of pig Latin. Made more popular by the song "Double Dutch Bus."

Jap—Equal to sap. Other similar words are: peon, mark, vic, crank, and lame.

Jordan's—Famous basketball player Michael Jordan has his own gym shoe line that cost one hundred and twenty dollars and up! These gym shoes are not only popular, but a fad in the ghetto. In fact, teenage girls sell their bodies for them and guys will pay the store an extra hundred to get the shoes a month early, before their due date. Yes, each pair that comes out has a due date, like a car!

Juice—Term used when someone has a lot of pull or clout in their neighborhood, crew, organization, or occupation. "Go talk to Kevin about your problem with those guys; he has a lot of juice, he can probably help you out."

Juke— The dances that one does to Chicago street **House** music.

Kitchen—Where the back of your head meets your neck and your hair is nappiest. The naps are often humorously referred to as buck shots (new growth). "Girl, you better do something to that kitchen soon, it's looking a little rough!"

Kyte—Letter or note. "I just got a kyte from my guy Rick, he's all good on that business."

Lamp— To lay back and relax, or chill.

Lick—Often referred to as "hit a lick" and having the same meaning as "bust a stain" and "come up." When one hits a lick, he does something where money can come out of the deal; he benefits from it.

Linoleum—Linoleum was carried around during the '80s for break dancing purposes.

Match—When someone in the organizations mess up (do something outside of the guidelines, whether while locked up or on the street), they get dealt with. Sometimes it's a mouth shot, if it's not that serious, but when it is more serious they get a match. They go in the bathroom or cell and their organization put the Foo Fops on them for the duration of a lighted match. Someone actually lights a match. and three or four people whoop the inmate until the match goes out! Often someone will get three or four matches, depending on how badly he messed up.

Mix—1. Songs mixed by a DJ that blend into one another, so as to keep the music coming. Often, House music is labeled by Chicagoans as "Mixture," the same as mainstream society has labeled Hip Hop as being Rap. 2. What is used to stretch your cocaine or heroin, in order to make more money.

Mixed—Someone who is blessed (fortunate) by having different nationalities in his or her makeup, giving one the diversity of culture, understanding, and outlook.

Mouth Shot—Violation given when one in an organization does something that is out of the guidelines or disrespectful.

Nigga—Street term for homie; a generalization for the word "man" (of any color).

Oh, that's what we on!?—Phrase quickly stated in response to someone who cases on you.

On the Bricks—Phrase used when describing "back in society" or "on the streets" while being incarcerated. "I'll be back out on the bricks next week, fam, I get out next Tuesday!"

Organizations—Terms used by Chicagoans (and others) when talking about our street gangs, because of how organized Folks and People are.

Pennies—Break dance move developed from the "helicopter" (windmill), except with no hands.

People—See Folks.

Phat—The equivalent of "bomb" or "dope." If something is phat, it's all that and a bag of chips!

Piece—1. Finished product of graffiti artwork. "That new piece that Frosty did is phat!" 2. A gun.

Player—Male or female who is open in their relationships (able to maintain—honestly—more than one relationship); being able to date exclusively; not being satisfied with one partner, yet being willing to let go if one of their partners finds someone they want to settle down with. A Player is a good man (or woman) who plays the field because they are comfortable doing so at that moment in their life. All players settle down when the time is right.

Plugged—To be down with the click; to fit in. In Chicago, one who's plugged means they're either Folks or People.

Point—In shooting craps, your point is what you have to make without crapping out.

Po Po's—The police or detectives. "Man, watch that strip, the po po's are coming down!"

Pop—To take Ecstasy. "C'mon, let's go pop two of them thangs, I'm ready to roll!"

Pop Locking—Cousin of break dance, where arms and body swings, rotates, claps, and points simultaneously, as Re-run did in *What's Happening?*

Popped Off—To get caught in the act by associates, a girlfriend, or the police; to get arrested and sent to jail.

Primo—Tobacco or marijuana laced with cocaine and smoked.

Quaker—Twenty-five dollars; also referred to as a "Quarter Horse."

Rap—Poetry. Lyrical form of expression that has now become mainstream through records. Though the industry has been exploited by society, the media, and the powers that be, it remains true in many places. In white-collar society, rap has been falsely confused with Hip Hop.

Raw—1. When referring to heroin, before adding mix. 2. Cocaine in its powder form, before being cooked into crack.

Real Talk—Street phrase used when describing a serious note. "Don't touch my car, I just got it washed! Don't have me bust your lip, fam, real talk!"

Renegade—When street organizations branch off and try to do their own thing, not complying with their bigger branch—and not giving a damn. They always get dealt with in the long run.

Roc—To wear something. "Man, let me roc that jersey tonight!"

Rocks—Cocaine broken down (already cooked) and ready to sell. 2. Diamonds.

Rollin'—Term used for feeling the affects of Ecstasy. "Look at Don, you can tell he's rollin'."

Runner—Most recently, an **extreme word** for bust down. A female who has sex with just about anyone because she can—and does!

S—Short for "Security," as in watching out for someone to make sure nothing goes wrong. "Put some S on that bathroom door while I give this fool two matches!"

Salty—To be upset at something or someone; to be pissed off. "I'm salty as hell at Eyvonne, she's playing damn games!"

Saw Buck—Ten dollars; also referred to as "saw head" or "Tension."

Script—To come up with a quick excuse or phony story, usually a fabrication or lie, so as to clear themselves. "Man, dig, Neicey gonna make up some phony-ass script about being out all night, I had to check her ass!"

Send Off—To be easily persuaded to do something or someone. A send off man is basically a flunky, and will show his ignorance to impress or fit in.

Serve—Selling drugs; also referred to as slanging, swerving, tippin' or working. 2. To win or put down someone in competition. "Ha ha, Chuck served you on those yo mama jokes!"

Set—1. A party. 2. Where you hang or live; the set that you claim is the area you're from or represent.

Shady—For someone to act wrongfully, in your perception of how they should act; also, a sneaky person whom you can't fully trust. "Trina played me shady yesterday, girl. She could have picked me up before she went to the shop."

Shake Down—For the officers of an institution (the penitentiary or county jail) to come in and thoroughly search your living quarters, as well as strip search.

Shank—Penitentiary weapon made from anything metal, used for fighting, often resulting in death. Other names are: candy bar, banger, tool, and sword,

Shyster—One who's slick, deceptive, and untrustworthy. Sneaky is too soft a word for a shyster.

Short—Being close to your **outdate** (going home from the county jail or penitentiary). "I'm getting short, man; I only got forty-five days left."

Show Love—To represent your organization, either by a handshake or throwing up a hand insignia from a distance.

Sick—For someone to be mentally sick because something happened to them that they feel was bad and made their predicament worse. "I can tell Donald is sick as hell since Vivian left him!"

Skitching—Winter street sport, where people hold onto the back of cars and busses using their feet as ski's to pull them through the snow.

Slam(s)—Expressing a story through poetry. Slam is more radiant and powerful than poems, because the artist explodes during his presentation, making it a magnificent performance.

Slick—One who has slipped by or gotten over on someone else.

Snitch—One who tells 5.0 someone else's business. Sometimes he does it if he's involved with the crime, in order to get a deal for his case. This also is called a "trick" or stool pigeon. If the case is already in court and the person does this for a deal, it's called "turning state's."

Snurfing- Sport similiar to water skiing (slolem) with one board on the snow.

Sporting—1. To pay someone else's way. 2. What you are wearing.

Sprung—When one is obsessed with another for their love, sex, or both! Sometimes two people can be sprung on each other.

Stacking—For one to put up his money until he reaches a certain amount. "I've been stacking my shit for three months now; I'm ready to go to the Lot."

Stalking—Sometimes the aftereffect of being sprung; to keep calling your lover, blowing up their pager or cell phone, often popping up unannounced.

Stole—The act of hitting someone unannounced; to sucker punch someone.

Strapped—1. To be carrying a gun. 2. For a male or female to be fully equipped with attractive body parts. "Look at Gina's ass! Damn, she's strapped!"

Strip—When one sets up shop (selling drugs on a block), the strip is what you have to watch, because this is where the cops will be coming from, 2. Known area where prostitutes walk back and fourth, selling their bodies; also referred to as the **Hoe Stroll**.

Stud- female lesbian that assumes the male role in the relationship. Previously reffered to as "Butch."

Stunner—This word has similar meanings, although they can be completely opposite. A stunner is similar to a baler—the ultimate baler! However, depending on how you use it, it could mean an imposter baler—a phony; the same as a "wannabe," someone having a Folex instead of a Rolex. "Did you see the rims on Zak's new truck? That brotha is a number-one stunner for real. Then the negative meaning of stunner: "Did you see them wannabe assassin rims? That vic knows he's a stunner!" So it can be either good or bad, depending on how you use it.

Sweatin'—1. For the police to keep monitoring an area in hopes of catching someone. 2. For a person to keep calling you or bothering you.

Sweet—Someone that is too easy to get over on. Often the phrase is "sweet as bear meat." "Hey, Jamie had her a sweet vic yesterday, she got seven hundred bucks!"

Table Tops—Break dance move where you're arched on your back and freeze.

Tagging—When a graffiti artist writes his name as a representation of himself or his crew.

Tech—To try and bring up an issue or point to win an argument or game. Often the tech will be used bogusly. "Man! Did you hear that tech Steve is trying to pull about stealing that car? I don't care how righteous he is, fuck him up!"

The Game—The game is cold, but it's fair. The game represents all that is done on the street to survive, get over, make money, hustle, eat, and live. Being in the game to youth is simply looked upon as selling drugs, which it is not. The game is a state of mind, it is a way of life, and it has offered you ways to survive without a nine-to-five job. Your money can be conjured legally out of thin air, which cannot be told for free. You will have to be a part of the game to understand this. The game is to be sold, not told.

Thomas Flares—break dance move based on technique of gymnast Kurt Thomas, where the legs are in open scissor formation and twirl 360 degrees. This move was invented for the pommel horse, but has now been taken to the floor.

Three Card Marley—Also called "Three Card Monte." Con game played with three cards where you have to find one (usually the ace). The catch is that the man cheats, and also uses a supposedly innocent bystander to promote his honesty (letting them win), but they are actually working together. The people that pull off this Three Card Marley stunt are true shysters.

Throwaways—Guns purchased strictly for the purpose of giving to the police so as to not catch a case. 2. A gun that is literally thrown away after doing a crime.

Throw Up—Basic graffiti done with no more than three colors; usually someone's initials, often done in bubble-style letters.

Tic for Tac—When someone feels as if they have to pay someone back for what they did, often related to relationships; revenge. "Okay bet, Joe, you want to play me with Maria! I could do tick for tack because it's going to hurt you worse, poppy!"

Ticking—Hip-hop dance move similar to animation, but slowed down and done with sharp, hard movements, as if an electric shock wave has gone through your body.

Tight—To be cool with or comfortable just the way you are. If you don't get high and someone offers you a joint, you would politely decline by saying, "Thanks, but no thanks, I'm tight." Also means something that looks good, sounds good, or is to your preference. "I love that radio, it's tight!"

Tippin'—This is more detailed than serving (and somewhat the aftereffect). When someone is tippin' they have become successful at serving, meaning that day, month, or year! They have a lot of money or material things to show for their serving. "I see that fat knot in your pocket, Greg! You been tippin' today. I know it!"

Trick—1. Date for a prostitute. 2. A peon or someone you have no respect for. 3. To tell on someone. "Look at Bobby talking to the police, he's tricking on Scott."

Triflin'—For someone to be nasty, dirty, or sneaky; to act wrongfully, as far as what we feel to be right; trife is used for an abbreviation. "That hoe Vikki is triflin'—she just slept with her baby's father's best friend!"

Trippin'—For one to act out of context for the situation; to get highly upset or act up about an issue or predicament.

ULON—"United Legion of One Nation." New term for Hip Hop, still using its five components: dance (break dancing being one of the strongest), DJing, MCing (Rapping, Poetry), graffiti art, and fashion (terms, styles, and clothes). However, with the change in name came a sixth component: political agenda. Since this new component added a deeper overtone and concept, a more serious name was sought to represent this movement. The old term Hip Hop was changed to ULON as people and organizations around the world embraced this new culture as the entity that it truly is.

Vamp—To jump on something or someone. "The po po's vamped on Carl yesterday!"

Vets—Females that are fifteen or more years your senior; short for veteran, and used when explaining your more mature, responsible woman.

Vic—Short for victim, used when talking about someone who's a pushover, not respected, or phony.

Violating—Penalty for someone messing up in their organization; to get dealt with.

Wanging—For your sound system to be bumpin'! Loud!

Water—**P.C.P** (Phencyclidine). Chemical and liquid substance used to make mint leaf or happy sticks; also called wikki or wack.

What—Meaning "period," as if you're challenging anyone to say something after what you've said—that's it, that's all. "Get the hell outta my way! I don't mess with you no more! What!"

Whip—Car. "Let me jump in my whip, I'll be there in a minute."

Woofin'—Someone talking shit that they can't back up; to put up a front.

Whoop—To get beat out of something or cheated; also called ganked. If someone sells you a whoop bag of cocaine, you've been swindled—it's probably dry wall.

Work—Drugs. "I gotta go pick up some work, I'll be back later."

Zoo Zoos and Wam Wams—Munchies, snacks, and food!

There was once a light at the end of a tunnel, you saw it, and you struggled to get to it. This book is dedicated to those who struggle to get to it, and to those who stand still—letting the light come to them. Sometimes we stand in what we believe to be darkness, though the light surrounds us. Keep on! Because whether you struggle to get to the light, or patiently await it—knowing it's there—you seek the light!

Thus you shall find it, thus it shall come...

Thus it shall come.